PLANTS vs. MEATS

THE HEALTH, HISTORY, AND ETHICS OF WHAT WE EAT

MEREDITH SAYLES HUGHES

TWENTY-FIRST CENTURY BOOKS / MINNEAPOLIS

TO MY LONGTIME COCONSPIRATOR IN ALL THINGS FOOD, TOM HUGHES: TEACHER, FOUNDER OF THE POTATO MUSEUM, AND COFOUNDER OF THE FOOD MUSEUM —M.S.H.

WITH SPECIAL THANKS TO EDITORIAL WHIZ PEG GOLDSTEIN, AND HER SIDEKICK, JACKIE-O. WITHOUT PEG'S INDEFATIGABLE WRESTLING SKILLS, THIS BOOK MIGHT NOT BE IN YOUR HANDS.
—M.S.H.

Twenty-First Century Books
A division of Lerner Publishing Group, Inc.
241 First Avenue North
Minneapolis, MN 55401 USA

For reading levels and more information, look up this title at www.lernerbooks.com.

Main body text set in Rotis Serif Std 10.5/15.
Typeface provided by Adobe Systems.

Library of Congress Cataloging-in-Publication Data

Hughes, Meredith Sayles.
    Plants vs. Meats: The Health, History, and Ethics of What We Eat / Meredith Sayles Hughes.
    pages cm
    ISBN 978-1-4677-8011-7 (lb : alk. paper) — ISBN 978-1-4677-9580-7 (eb PDF)
    1. Vegetarian foods. 2. Vegetarianism. 3. Diet. 4. Food—Social aspects. I. Title.
  TX391.H84 2015
  641.5'636—dc23   2015007494

Manufactured in the United States of America
1 –PC – 12/31/15

CONTENTS

AUTHOR'S NOTE

MANY CHEFS, FOOD WRITERS, AND OTHER VETERANS OF VEGETARIANISM turned veggie during the 1960s and 1970s. Peter Singer's 1975 book *Animal Liberation*, about the cruelty of industrial farming, did it for me. I was living in Brussels, Belgium—a place abundant in excellent cooking. And I loved to eat. As a little girl on family excursions to restaurants, I had always ordered steak. But that book, which I read as an adult in 1975, stopped me cold.

While in Europe, my husband and I began to move away from meat, beginning with chicken. The reason was named Harold the Hen, a pet bird who lived with us after being born with crooked feet in a school chick experiment gone wrong. We adopted her, misnamed her based on ignorance, and fell in love. Harold hobbled in and out of our kitchen freely, from her house in our back garden. She sunbathed with us on the rare occasion the sun shone in northern Europe, helped weed our veggie garden, and ferociously hunted bugs in our ivy beds.

One day, after picking up Harold and hugging her scrawny little chest, I washed my hands and prepared to roast a chicken I had just bought from the local butcher. I stared at the small bird, cold and dead on my counter, and realized then and there that I could not eat something so akin, exactly akin, to dear Harold. That chicken went to our landlady instead. We quit eating animals "cold chicken," you might say.

Today, however, after forty-plus years of eating mostly veggies, fish, and full-fat cheeses and butter, we have decided to eat more beef and poultry. The science has convinced us of the health benefits of meats.

Several well-known chefs and food writers have undertaken similar changes in diet. They have evolved into omnivorous eaters after decades of vegetarianism. This group includes Deborah Madison. In the 1970s, she launched the all-veggie San Francisco restaurant Greens, which is still going strong. Madison is the author of many books, including the bible of veg, *Vegetarian Cooking for Everyone* (1997). In her 2013 book *Vegetable Literacy*, Madison reveals the richness of the edible plant world. She does not push for strict adherence to any one diet. Instead, the book is about the joy, beauty, taste, and goodness of cooking and eating vegetables, especially those grown by you or those grown nearby. In a 2014 interview with the *Washington Post*, Madison said, "We're not interested in fundamental lifestyles of vegetarianism and veganism. . . . It's not about saying no to this or no to that. It can be if you want, or it can be that you simply want to eat some vegetables."

In a 2013 interview, Mollie Katzen, whose *Moosewood Cookbook* (1974) and other cookbooks became classic primers on how to cook veggies, says that she advocates neither for vegetarianism nor meat eating. Based in Berkeley, California, Katzen is involved with Healthy Kitchens, Healthy Lives, a symposium that blends nutritional information with good cooking. She writes, "I just think that what we eat is a personal choice. I wish people would just enjoy it and not be dogmatic about it. . . . I'm not a pure vegetarian myself, and I don't like to defend my food choices. I love to eat healthy foods that are well prepared."

This book will help you make thoughtful decisions about what you eat. Whether you choose to be a vegetarian, a vegan, a carnivore, an omnivore, or another type of eater, I hope that you too decide to eat healthy, delicious foods.

1-ARIANS

"WHEN EATING BAMBOO SPROUTS, REMEMBER THE PERSON WHO PLANTED THEM."
—Chinese proverb

VEGETARIANS, PESCATARIANS, AND VEGANS; flexitarians, fruitarians, foragers, and raw foodists; omnivores, carnivores, and locavores. What is the best, healthiest, and most ethical way to eat?

We all need food, the fuel that keeps us moving and productive. But what we choose to eat and how we choose to prepare it is up to us. And it appears that in the twenty-first century, more and more Americans are choosing to eat more and more vegetables and fruits. Americans who follow a vegetarian diet eat no meat at all, which means no red meat, poultry, seafood, or the flesh of any other animal. Within the vegetarian category are many variations. For instance, pescatarians eat fish but not beef, pork, or chicken. Flexitarians, sometimes known as cautious carnivores, are people whose diet is largely plant-based but who occasionally eat meat, fish, or other animal products.

Vegans eat neither meat nor any other products derived from animals. This includes eggs, milk, cheese, and other dairy products. Raw foodists eat mostly uncooked food, and most of them are vegans. Fruitarians, another group falling in the vegan column, mainly eat fruit, usually uncooked. (All vegetables produced from seeds, including tomatoes, peppers, and avocados, are considered fruits.)

AND -ISMS

People who live in wealthy nations such as the United States usually have an abundance of food to choose from. But what are the healthiest choices, and which choices best fit with your values?

According to a 2013 Public Policy Polling survey, 6 percent of US adult respondents described themselves as vegetarian, while 7 percent claimed to be vegan. *Vegetarian Times* magazine reports that 7.3 million Americans are vegetarians.

TIME FOR TERMS

Beyond vegetarianism, Americans can choose from among many other ways of eating. A carnivore is a meat eater. Your cat is one of these. Your Venus flytrap too is a carnivore, ingesting the insects it attracts to its landing pad. An omnivore is a person or animal that eats everything—plants, dairy products, fish, shellfish, and meat. Your dog is one of these. The omnivore category also includes those who pursue the paleo diet

IN THE RAW

A large raw food gathering takes place in the Adirondack Mountains of New York State. The weeklong Woodstock Fruit Festival, held in August since 2011, attracts several hundred fruitarians and raw foodists each year. They come to relax, talk with raw food gurus, romp in the woods, swim in the lake, and eat unlimited quantities of fresh fruits and vegetables.

Fiction writer and essayist Alexandra Kleeman attended the 2014 event. She wrote, "You burn your meals quickly and are hungry again soon. . . . I wasn't full. . . . I didn't know how much I'd have to eat, or how much time I'd have to spend peeling, tearing, chewing." She warned: "Fruit, for all its excellent qualities, is low in protein, calcium, vitamin B12, zinc, Omega-3 and 6 fatty acids, iodine, and vitamin D. Sticking to the diet long term can result in dangerous deficiencies that many fruitarians try to ward off with nutritional testing and vitamin injections." Harvard University biologist Richard Wrangham notes that many raw foodists are underweight. In one study of raw foodists, half the women had stopped menstruating—a sign that they were not only underweight but also malnourished.

(eating only the types of foods, such as meats, fish, nuts, fruits, and veggies, thought to be available to our prehuman ancestors), as well as families sitting at the dinner table who eat whatever the household cook has come up with.

Jessica Prentice, a food writer from the San Francisco Bay Area in California, coined the term *locavore*. In the summer of 2005, she and several other women challenged people in the Bay Area to eat only foods raised within a 100-mile (161-kilometer) radius of San Francisco for one month. Although the 100-mile designation is not a hard-and-fast rule, locavores try to eat locally produced foods whenever possible. Eating this way supports local farmers and food businesses. It can be a smart health decision too, because foods deliver their full nutritional value when eaten fresh off the farm—less so when they're processed, stored, and transported by refrigerated trucks across the country or by ships across the ocean. If you're a dedicated locavore in the United States, your food choices might be limited. For example, you might see bananas at the grocery store, but most likely they were grown more than 100 miles away and shipped in, since bananas grow only in tropical areas. So a locavore wouldn't eat them. Of course, if you live in tropical Florida or Hawaii, or in a banana-growing region in India, Asia, Central America, or South America, then bananas might be a staple of your locavore diet.

Foragers walk through woods and fields, looking for wild edible plants. They might come across wild mushrooms, leeks, berries, or fruiting apple trees. They might eat barberries, red fruits that grow in winter and are easily spotted in snowy places. Nettles and henbits, members of the mint family, can also be foraged in winter. Foragers might also gather rhizomes, the main underground stems of certain types of plants. Ginger, turmeric, and bamboo are examples of edible rhizomes. Those who prefer to forage at home can plant highbush cranberries, quinces, mulberries, and currants and forage right in the backyard.

WHY GO VEG?

Many people become vegetarian for health reasons, believing that high-fiber, low-fat vegetables and grains are healthier than high-fat beef, pork, and chicken. Other vegetarians choose the diet for ethical reasons. In the urbanized twenty-first century, most of us do not have to kill the food we eat, whether a pheasant in the wild or a Black Angus steer grazing in a green pasture. In our plastic-wrapped era of supermarket meat sales, we buy a chop but do not see the slaughtered pig from which it was cut. We deep-fry chicken wings coated in tasty crumbs, but we do not envision the alert hen who, before her slaughter, flapped her wings as she descended from her nest. Except that some of us do. Many people see animals as soulful, sensitive, and dignified beings and don't want to be responsible for their deaths—which is why they decide to eat fewer creatures and more plants. That's the ethical reason for vegetarianism.

Ethical simply means: Is this action or behavior right or wrong? A

Consumers are accustomed to purchasing cuts of meat wrapped in sterile plastic packaging. But before we can eat animals, they must be slaughtered and butchered. Here, sides of beef hang in a meat locker.

vegetarian typically thinks that killing animals for food is wrong. A vegan believes that it is wrong to exploit any animals for human use—so vegans do not eat eggs, milk, cheese, or other dairy products. In addition, many vegans refuse to wear leather (made from animal hides) or use any other product derived from the bodies of animals. Some believe that eating vegan is the healthiest option. But most people become vegan for ethical, not health, reasons.

In general, only people in wealthy nations can afford meat, while millions of others around the globe rely instead on grain-based diets and millions more are undernourished. In the United States, 40 percent of corn goes into the production of ethanol, a type of alcohol that is used to power vehicles. Another 36 percent feeds cattle, hogs, and chickens that will be eaten by people. Many vegetarians and vegans argue that were we to use corn and other crops to feed humans, instead of using them for fuel and to feed food animals, we could more efficiently feed Earth's seven-plus billion people. We could also save freshwater—a dwindling natural resource—by moving away from meat-based diets. It takes an estimated 441 gallons (1,669 liters) of water to produce 1 pound (0.5 kilograms) of beef. This includes water the animal drinks, water to irrigate pastureland, water to grow corn to feed the animal, and water involved in processing the meat. By contrast one pound of pasta made from wheat requires about half as much water—222 gallons (840 liters). One pound of potatoes requires just 34 gallons (129 liters) of water.

In the United States and around the world, most cattle, pigs, and other food animals are raised in feedlots. Vegans, vegetarians, and others note that these animals are fed on grains, particularly corn, which are not natural foods for them. Such grains can damage the animals' digestive and reproductive systems. These grains are also laced with growth hormones and antibiotics, which quickly fatten up the animals for slaughter but which can also pose health problems in humans. For instance, the overuse of antibiotics in farm animals can create superbugs, disease-causing bacteria that are resistant to medications. And some studies have linked the use of growth hormones in animals to an increased risk for certain cancers in people who eat the meat. In addition, grains used to feed farm animals are frequently grown with massive amounts of chemical fertilizers and pesticides, which can contaminate soil and water and also, many experts say, make food products unsafe to eat.

Vegetarians and vegans are also concerned with animal welfare. At feedlots, cattle and other animals are crowded together with no room to roam. Some livestock are locked in pens. Critics view crowding as cruelty, since it leads to stress and the spread of diseases among animals. Animal rights activists also object to brutal methods used to slaughter food animals at commercial slaughterhouses. The cruel treatment of animals on factory farms and at slaughterhouses has spurred many people to become vegetarians. Vegans explain that even animals that are not initially killed for food—such as hens raised for their eggs and dairy cattle raised to give milk—are eventually slaughtered after they are no longer productive egg layers or milk makers.

ARE WE OMNIVORES?

Modern humans are descended from mainly herbivorous, or plant-eating, ancestors from Africa. These early ancestors lived in trees and survived by eating fruit snagged from those trees and other wild-growing plant foods.

Anthropologists (scientists who study human cultures) tell us that once our early ancestors moved to a life on the ground, they broadened their diets. The first humans were hunter-gatherers. They ate whatever food they could trap, dig from the ground, gather from bushes, snare, corner, pluck, pick, or scavenge. They often traveled from place to place, looking for game and fresh supplies of wild plants.

In prehistoric times, in societies around the globe, humans used spears, clubs, and bows and arrows to hunt animals for food. Some early humans painted or carved hunting scenes on the walls of caves and cliff faces. This painting, created by ancient San people, is a feature in uKhahlamba Drakensberg Park in South Africa.

GREAT AND INVENTIVE APES

To learn about the diets of early humans, many scientists study chimpanzees *(right)*, which are more closely related to humans than any other animals. Chimps enjoy eating meat, according to acclaimed primatologist Jane Goodall, who has noted that chimps hunt, kill, and eat smaller mammals. They also gobble up fruits, leaves, nuts, tubers, and seeds, as well as insects.

In June 2015, researchers at the Jane Goodall Institute's Tchimpounga Chimpanzee Rehabilitation Center in the Republic of the Congo were surprised to discover that chimps prefer the taste of cooked food over raw food. In a study at the sanctuary, chimps chose cooked sweet potatoes over uncooked sweet potatoes 90 percent of the time, even when they had to wait to eat them. This preference for cooked foods might have been what led our human ancestors to harness fire for cooking one million or more years ago.

Abundant evidence—such as butchery marks on ancient animal bones—suggests that early humans ate meat as early as 2.6 million years ago. Scientists say that early human species pounded open animal bones, so they could eat the marrow inside, and sliced meat off bones with sharp tools. Early humans probably also ate insects. Termites, ants, and other insects would have been a good source of protein, especially when other protein-rich food was scarce. A study by anthropologists at Washington University in Saint Louis, Missouri, suggests that protein provided by insects may have contributed to the growth of the early human brain.

Fire sprang up at random from lightning strikes, so the earliest humans used fire for cooking as they came upon it. Once people learned how to intentionally create a fire, by striking two stones together to make a spark, for instance, they could reliably cook food daily. Different groups learned to make fire at different times in different parts of the world. *Homo erectus*, a species that lived in Africa between 1.89 million and 143,000 years ago, may have been the first group on Earth to create cooking fires.

Harvard University anthropologist Richard Wrangham explains that humans absorb nutrients, such as proteins, from cooked meat more easily than from raw meat. In addition, cooking makes starchy, carbohydrate-heavy foods, such as potatoes and yams, easier to digest. So after early humans began cooking meat and plant foods, their nutrition improved. And as humans gained more nutrients from cooked foods, their brains grew larger. People became smarter. In addition, scientists point out that raw meat—especially when scavenged in the wild—is often teeming with harmful bacteria. Cooking kills off much of these bacteria, so cooked meat is safer to eat than raw meat. By cooking meat, our human ancestors cut down their chances of getting foodborne illnesses.

Our jaws changed with the introduction of cooking as well. Anthropologists point out that human teeth and jaws were originally quite large, suited to chewing tough raw meat and fibrous plants. Over thousands of years, as people ate more cooked meat and vegetables, their molars and jaws became smaller, more suited to chewing softer cooked foods. In addition, the human gut—or intestines—eventually became shorter, because food that has been cut into small pieces and cooked takes less time to digest than large pieces of uncooked food.

OUR CLOSE RELATIONS

Neanderthals, early humans who lived in Europe and central Asia between 150,000 and 35,000 years ago, were omnivores. Anthropologists believe that Neanderthals hunted for large and small game. Plants were on the Neanderthal menu as well. Anthropologists have found bits of cooked

THE CAVE MAN DIET

Some nutritionists say that the human digestive system is not well suited to processing domesticated grains. Grains can cause intestinal bloating and can overload the bloodstream with sugar (since the carbohydrates in grains break down into sugar in the body). Based on the idea that grains are unhealthy, some people have taken up the paleo diet—eating as they believe our hunter-gatherer ancestors did during the Paleolithic era (2.6 million years ago to about 10,000 years ago.) Hunter-gatherers during the Paleolithic era, which ended with the development of agriculture, would have eaten mostly small animals, fish, shellfish, fruits, tubers, seeds, and nuts.

Loren Cordain is the self-proclaimed founder of the paleo movement. Another paleo champion, Michelle Tam, promotes paleo-style eating with a colorful blog called *Nom Nom Paleo*. Here's a list of approved and forbidden foods from Cordain's website:

OKAY TO EAT	NOT OKAY TO EAT
Eggs	Cereal grains, such as wheat, corn, and rice
Fish and other seafood	Dairy
Fresh fruits and veggies	Legumes (including peanuts)
Healthful oils (olive, walnut, flaxseed, macadamia, avocado, and coconut oil)	Potatoes
	Processed foods
Meats from animals raised on grass	Refined (processed) sugar
Nuts and seeds	Refined vegetable oils
	Salt

grains in the teeth of a Neanderthal skeleton, as well as evidence of plants in fossilized, fifty-thousand-year-old Neanderthal poop, more scientifically known as coprolite. Scientists from the Massachusetts Institute of Technology analyzed coprolite samples from a Neanderthal campsite on the Mediterranean coast in Spain. The samples revealed that meat dominated the Neanderthal diet, along with "significant amounts of plant-derived" material. One scientist surmised that the plants were a mix of berries, nuts, and root vegetables. In a different study, Luca Fiorenza, an anthropologist at the University of New England in New South Wales, Australia, examined teeth from Neanderthals found in Italy. His studies revealed that they ate shellfish, seeds, and wild plants.

AGRICULTURE ON PURPOSE

In different parts of the world, between seven and ten thousand years ago, hunter-gatherers began to purposely scatter seeds in certain spots in the spring and return to these sites in late summer or early fall to harvest the ripe plants. Slowly, with the development of deliberate agriculture, family groups became more sedentary, eventually settling into full-time farming communities. They planted seeds, and they harvested, stored, and ate what they grew. The first domesticated grains—those that were adapted for human use—were barley in the Middle East, corn in the Americas, and rice in Asia.

BREAD OR BEER?

People first planted grains to more easily obtain food, right? Actually, some scientists argue that the goal was to create fermented (alcoholic) drinks, such as beer. Growing grain is hard work that involves not only planting but also irrigation, harvesting, and threshing (separating the seeds from the plants). Some anthropologists say that early farmers might have been more motivated to do that work by the desire for strong drink than by the desire for food.

In addition, fermented beverages were safer to drink than water in ancient times. Before the modern era of indoor plumbing and water treatment plants, people often used nearby streams and lakes as toilets and then drew their drinking water from the same streams and lakes. In this way, many water supplies became contaminated with pathogens, such as viruses or bacteria. Fermentation killed these pathogens. Beer also gave people some of the same nutrients as bread, including B vitamins, niacin, and zinc.

WHAT ÖTZI ATE

In 1991 hikers in the mountains of northern Italy found the well-preserved body of a fifty-three-hundred-year-old man *(below)*, frozen in deep ice. Scientists named him Ötzi and have been minutely studying his body since its discovery. Scientists have done tests on the deoxyribonucleic acid (DNA), or genetic material, in Ötzi's intestines and colon to determine his last meal. The tests have showed that it consisted of red deer, ibex (a species of wild goat), and grains.

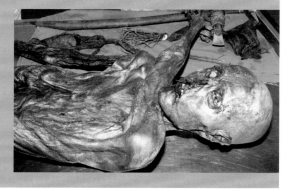

Along with the establishment of farming came the domestication, or taming, of wild animals for human use and consumption. Domesticated animals provided ancient farmers with meat, wool, eggs, and milk. They also helped farmers work by pulling plows and carrying heavy loads. The first domestication of animals for food took place in the Middle East about 9000 BCE (before the common era), when farmers began to raise goats for meat and wool. Then came pigs, cattle, and chickens. In the Americas, ancient peoples domesticated llamas, alpacas, guinea pigs, and turkeys, which they slaughtered and ate. Ancient Americans also used dogs to pull sleds and llamas to carry heavy loads. The farmers also wove garments from alpaca hair.

2 "THEY WILL BE

RELIGIONS FLOURISHED IN THE ANCIENT WORLD,
and each one provided different dietary guidelines for followers. In ancient
India, a religion called Hinduism began to take shape in the eighteenth
century BCE. Hinduism's far-flung ancient sects and groups opposed
violence against animals, and many of its adherents were vegetarians.
The early Hindus lavished gifts of food on their many gods and goddesses,
and to be pure, this food had to be plant-based. Hindus were not required
to be vegetarians, but scholars say that ancient Hindu farmers were not
likely to kill and eat cows and other animals that they needed to perform
farm labor. In modern times, the cow remains the most revered animal in
Hinduism, and for this reason, Hindus do not eat beef. Hindus live all over
the world, and modern India has more Hindus—and more vegetarians—than
any other country on Earth.

Between 1200 and 1000 BCE, the followers of a teacher called Zoroaster
established Zoroastrianism in a region that would later become modern-
day Iran. A Zoroastrian text is often quoted as proof that Zoroaster and his
followers favored plants over meat. The text quotes Zoroastrian high priest
Atrupat-e Emetan as saying, "Be plant eaters, O you men, so that you may
live long. Keep away from the body of the cattle, and deeply reckon that
Ohrmazd, the Lord, has created plants in great number for helping cattle
and men." Zoroastrianism was a dominant religion in the ancient Middle
East, but in the twenty-first century, its adherents number under two
hundred thousand, and they are not required to be vegetarians.

YOURS FOR FOOD"

Many ancient religions forbade the eating of certain kinds of animals. The ancient Hindus usually did not eat cows, since they were considered sacred. A cow and calf are prominent in this eighteenth-century painting, which features a Hindu god and goddess.

Jainism is a religion established in northern India in the sixth century BCE. Its members are strict vegetarians who believe in harming no living beings. Modern-day Jains go so far as to wear masks to avoid inhaling bugs. Buddhism, a religious practice originating in India around 500 BCE, is widespread throughout modern Asia. The religion's founder, Siddhartha Gautama, was not a vegetarian, but he told his followers not to kill any living thing. Some Buddhists have interpreted this message to mean that they should not eat meat. In modern times, many Buddhists are vegetarians.

The Islamic religion, which is widely practiced in the Middle East, Southeast Asia, and other parts of the world, was established by the prophet Muhammad in the seventh century CE. Islam forbids the eating of pork and of any animal that is not halal, or slaughtered according

EAT LIKE AN EGYPTIAN

French scientists have examined mummies (preserved remains) of Egyptians who lived between 3500 BCE and 600 CE. The scientists have measured carbon levels in the mummies' teeth, bones, and hair to determine what kinds of foods they ate. (Plants take in carbon during photosynthesis, when they convert the sun's energy into food. Carbons, which decay very slowly, end up in the bodies of people and animals that eat plants.) The researchers discovered that these ancient Egyptians had a largely vegetarian diet, eating large amounts of wheat and barley but very little meat or fish.

to Islamic law. Islam includes a number of other dietary restrictions. For example, Muslims (those who practice Islam) are forbidden to drink alcohol. Combining elements of Hinduism and Islam, Sikhism originated in the sixteenth century in the Punjab region of modern-day India and Pakistan. Early Sikh leaders were concerned about cruelty to both plants and animals. In this passage from a Sikh text, a guru laments the suffering of sugarcane:

> Look, and see how the sugar-cane is cut down. After cutting away its branches, its feet are bound together into bundles, and then, it is placed between the wooden rollers and crushed.
>
> What punishment is inflicted upon it! Its juice is extracted and placed in the cauldron; as it is heated, it groans and cries out.
>
> And then, the crushed cane is collected and burnt in the fire below.

Guru Nanak, the founder of Sikhism, established vegetarian community kitchens in the Punjab. At these kitchens, anyone, poor or rich, could receive a simple, free meal. Sikhism still flourishes in the Punjab and in other places around the world, including the United States. The Sikh initiative of feeding the hungry continues in the twenty-first century.

For instance, after a giant tsunami hit South Asian nations in 2004 and after Hurricane Katrina hit New Orleans, Louisiana, in 2005, Sikh kitchens helped feed survivors of both disasters.

BIBLE STORIES

The Hebrew Bible is a collection of tales composed by different writers in the Middle East between about 1000 and 165 BCE. It is a sacred text to both Judaism and Christianity. Its various books tell people not to eat certain foods. The first forbidden food was an apple growing in the Garden of Eden, home to Adam and Eve, the Bible's first man and woman. According to the book of Genesis, the first book of the Bible, Adam and Eve could not resist the apple, so God exiled them from Eden. (Food historians point out that apples, native to China, did not grow in the ancient Middle East at all, so it's much more likely the fruit that Adam and Eve would have eaten was a pomegranate or a banana.)

Other food prohibitions are found in the book of Leviticus, the third book of the Bible. Leviticus advises:

> Whatever parts the hoof and is cloven-footed and chews the cud, among the animals, you may eat. Nevertheless, among those that chew the cud or part the hoof, you shall not eat these: The camel, because it chews the cud but does not part the hoof, is unclean to you. And the rock badger, because it chews the cud but does not part the hoof, is unclean to you. And the hare, because it chews the cud but does not part the hoof, is unclean to you. And the pig, because it parts the hoof and is cloven-footed but does not chew the cud, is unclean to you. You shall not eat any of their flesh, and you shall not touch their carcasses; they are unclean to you.

This meant that cattle were okay to eat, but pigs and rabbits were out. According to other Bible passages, large, abundant meaty insects, such as locusts, katydids, crickets, and grasshoppers, were acceptable foods. Creatures living in water that lacked fins or scales, such as clams,

The Seventh-day Adventists are a Christian religious organization, formally established in Michigan in 1863. Many Adventists are vegetarians. They also avoid the foods prohibited in Leviticus. So too do many observant modern-day Jews, who call the practice keeping kosher.

mussels, and oysters, were definitely out. Why were some critters deemed clean and others unclean? The Bible gives few precise explanations, but modern scholars have some theories. For instance, camels might have been forbidden food in biblical times because they were needed as work animals. Pigs might have been forbidden because they ate too much food in comparison to the amount of meat they yielded. The Bible does say straight away that plants are intended to nourish humans. According to Genesis, God said to the first humans, "I give you every seed-bearing plant on the face of the whole earth and every tree that has fruit with seed in it. They will be yours for food."

Then came Noah. According to Genesis, Noah and his family, along with samples of Earth's birds and land animals (two each or seven each—depending on the kind of animal), all crowded together in a wooden ship called the ark for forty days and forty nights. On the ark, they were able to survive a major flood that wiped out the rest of humanity. Afterward, God gave Noah mastery over every living thing. He decreed, "Everything that lives and moves about will be food for you. Just as I gave you the green plants, I now give you everything." (The first thing Noah did on dry land was to plant a vineyard, so score one for plants there.)

Christianity, based on the teachings of the Hebrew Bible and the teachings of a Jewish religious leader named Jesus, emerged in the ancient Middle East in the first century CE. Early church leaders decreed that Christians should not eat meat on Fridays, the day of Jesus's death, as a way of remembering his suffering. So fish on Fridays was the norm for Christians—particularly Catholics—for centuries. At the Second Vatican Council, a meeting of Catholic leaders in the early 1960s, church leaders dropped the ban on meat eating on Fridays, but many Catholics still follow the rule, especially during Lent, a period leading up to Easter.

THE AMERICAN WAY

The ancient Americas nurtured some vegetarians. In North, South, and Central America, indigenous peoples raised vegetables and fruits, including tomatoes, chiles, avocados, beans, potatoes, corn, cacao (from which comes chocolate), pineapples, and much more. In Mesoamerica (Mexico and Central America), Mayan and Aztec farmers cultivated corn, which they revered. Mayan and Aztec children ate mostly corn during their first ten years of life. People prepared corn in a variety of ways in ancient Mesoamerica. They ground it into meal and formed it into pancakes,

Corn was sacred to the ancient Aztecs, who lived in Mesoamerica (Mexico and Central America) during the 1400s and early 1500s. This page from the *Codex Féjerváry-Mayer*, an Aztec manuscript, shows corn as a humanlike being sitting on the ground. In the top left picture, the corn plant withers under the attention of a god called the Lord of Jewels. In the top right picture, the corn is healthy as the Aztec rain goddess waters it.

similar to modern-day tortillas. They also ate cooked corn kernels in soup and porridge and fresh off the cob.

Most Indian tribes in North America were omnivores. People fished and hunted small and large animals, depending on where they lived, but their diets were also vegetable-heavy. Most tribes cultivated corn, beans, and squash, a practice that spread north from Mexico around 1300 BCE and eventually across most of North America. Each tribe had its own foodways, depending on the types of plants that grew in the region. For instance, among the Choctaw Indians of the southeastern United States, "The principal food, eaten daily from earthen pots, was a vegetarian stew containing corn, pumpkin and beans," according to Choctaw historian Rita Laws. "The bread was made from corn and acorns. Other common favorites were roasted corn and corn porridge." Indian tribes in the Great Lakes region harvested wild rice, berries, and other wild plants. On the plateau northwest of the Rocky Mountains, Indians gathered bitterroot, wild carrots, and wild onions, among other plants. In the Northeast, tribes ate a lot of maple sugar, obtained from the sap of maple trees, which was used to sweeten breads, stews, and teas. Acorns, which could be ground into flour and used to prepare soup, mush, biscuits, and bread, were a staple food for tribes in California. All these foods complemented diets that were heavy on fish and game—when it could be had.

ON THE MATTER OF ANIMALS

One of the earliest arguments in the Western world for a plant-centered diet was put forth by the ancient Greek mystic and mathematician Pythagoras, who lived in the sixth century BCE. He believed that after people died, their souls returned in new forms, possibly as animals. So he said that people should not eat animals if they were uncomfortable with the notion of eating a person trapped in, say, a lamb's body. He also believed that killing animals explained humankind's violence against other people. He wrote, "As long as men massacre animals, they will kill each other." Aristotle, a Greek philosopher and scientist who lived in the fourth century

BCE, disagreed. He wrote, "Plants are created for the sake of animals, and animals for the sake of men."

Leonardo da Vinci, an Italian painter, thinker, and inventor of the fifteenth and sixteenth centuries, felt that humans were the cruelest animals of all. He bought birds and chickens from vendors and freed them so that they would not be purchased, slaughtered, and eaten. Dutch philosopher and physician Bernard Mandeville was also opposed to the killing of animals. He wrote in 1714, "We are born with a Repugnancy to the killing, and consequently the eating of Animals."

British philosopher Jeremy Bentham (1748–1832) advocated for women's rights and the abolition of slavery. He opposed the death penalty and favored the lifting of laws that criminalized homosexuality. He also opposed cruelty toward animals. Some people of his era argued that since animals could not think and communicate like humans, they did not deserve humane treatment. But Bentham countered, "The question is not, Can they reason? nor, Can they talk? but, Can they suffer?"

> "THE QUESTION IS NOT, CAN [ANIMALS] REASON? NOR, CAN THEY TALK? BUT, CAN THEY SUFFER?"
> —Jeremy Bentham

American inventor and statesman Benjamin Franklin avoided eating meat. He addressed the pursuit of vegetarianism with typical humor in his autobiography, published in 1793:

In my first Voyage from Boston, being becalm'd off Block Island, our people set about catching Cod & hawl'd up a great many. Hitherto I had stuck to my Resolution of not eating animal Food, and on this Occasion, I consider'd, with my Master Tryon, the taking every Fish as a kind of unprovoked Murder, since none of them had or ever could do us any Injury that might justify the Slaughter.—All this seem'd very reasonable.—But I had formerly been a great Lover of Fish, & when this came hot out of the Frying Pan, it smelt admirably well. I balanc'd some time between Principle and Inclination: till I recollected that, when the Fish were opened, I saw smaller Fish taken out of their stomachs:—Then, thought I, if you eat one another, I don't see why we mayn't eat you. So I din'd upon Cod very heartily and continu'd to eat with other People, returning only now & then occasionally to a vegetable Diet. So convenient a thing it is to be a reasonable Creature, since it enables one to find or make a Reason for everything one has a mind to do.

Thomas Jefferson, third president of the United States and an avid plant collector, was a meticulous note-keeping gardener on Monticello, his estate in Virginia. He also was decidedly a plant-based eater. As he put it in the early nineteenth century, "I have lived temperately, eating little animal food, and that . . . as a condiment for the vegetables, which constitute my principal diet."

A TERM OF THEIR OWN

The term *vegetarian* did not actually appear in print until the mid-nineteenth century. In 1842 the British journal the *Healthian* noted, "There is generally with vegetarians, and especially fruit eaters, a calmness and even sweetness of temper, and we believe also a clearness of reason, that are highly desirable for humanity, and for health."

American educator Bronson Alcott, the father of Louisa May Alcott, who wrote about their family in *Little Women* (1868–1869) and other works, was a vegetarian for ethical reasons. He ate no animal products at all and was a vegan before the word existed. Born in 1799, he also was an advocate of rights for women, an opponent of slavery, and an educational reformer. Englishman James Pierrepont Greaves started a school outside of London and named it Alcott House, after Bronson Alcott. He was determined to feed his students plant-based foods, along with new ideas. His efforts led to the creation of Britain's Vegetarian Society in 1847.

By 1848 vegetarianism had become a popular cause in the United Kingdom and the United States. The movement was ripe fruit for satirists, wordsmiths, and punsters. Holden's *Dollar Magazine*, published in New York, wrote with humor in 1848,

The vegetable eaters, who, a few years since, made so much noise amongst us, being stirred up by Dr. Graham [an American health reformer, for whom the graham cracker is named] have lately sprouted up in great numbers in England. They are there called Vegetarians . . . and have recently been having vegetable banquets all over England; and we should not be astonished if, by and by, we hear talk of the roast potatoes, instead of the roast beef of old England.

American writer Henry David Thoreau, a nineteenth-century friend of Bronson Alcott's, was an on and off vegetarian. In his 1854 book *Walden*, he wrote: "Whatever my own practice may be, I have no doubt that it is a part of the destiny of the human race, in its gradual improvement, to leave off eating animals, as surely as the savage tribes have left off eating each other when they came in contact with the more civilised."

DIET REFORMERS IN AMERICA

One of the founders of the American Vegetarian Society in 1850, Sylvester Graham, advocated a largely vegetarian diet that included butter and cheese. He said that food should be chewed slowly and thoroughly. Graham also advocated eating whole grains. In this era, white flour was a status symbol for the wealthy. Making white flour involved multiple grindings and siftings, and rich people had their servants do the work. This processing removed many of the vitamins and most of the fiber from the flour, making it less nutritious than brown flour, although its shelf life was longer. Graham, on the other hand, created brown flour from unsifted whole grains and urged his followers in Massachusetts to make a hearty and nutritious bread from the flour. His name lives on in the twenty-first century in graham crackers, which he developed in 1829.

J. H. Kellogg was another American food reformer. After studying medicine, Kellogg took over the running of a sanatorium (a combination health spa-hospital) in Battle Creek, Michigan. In his efforts to provide healthier food for his patients, he developed a plant-based cereal called cornflakes. He started a company to produce them in the late 1890s with

At his sanatorium in Battle Creek, Michigan, J. H. Kellogg promoted a vegetarian diet, fresh air, sunshine, and regular exercise for good health. This photo, taken around the beginning of the twentieth century, shows sanatorium patients doing breathing exercises.

his brother, Will Kellogg. The brothers eventually disagreed on the use of sugar in cornflakes. Astute businessman Will was in favor of adding sugar. He thought a sugared product would sell better. Will was correct. In 1906 he formed a new cereal business, which later became known as the Kellogg Company.

FLOUR POWER

The modern surge in plant-based eating truly began in the United States of the 1960s and the 1970s. Opposed to US involvement in the Vietnam War (1957–1975) and the conservative social and political views of their parents, many young people of this era became hippies. Some of them "dropped out" of conventional society, forming group living spaces called communes, going "back to the land" to grow their own food, and creating food-buying cooperatives that sold local and organic foods. Many became vegetarians.

DOING WITHOUT

During World War I (1914–1918), Americans on the home front ate much less meat—and not for ethical or health reasons. The US government wanted to provide as much meat as possible to US troops fighting overseas and to malnourished civilians in parts of war-torn Europe. During the war, the US Food Administration asked families to voluntarily give up meat on Mondays and wheat on Wednesdays. Millions of Americans did so.

During World War II (1939–1945), to provide food, fabric, metal, and other goods to the military, the US government rationed many foods, clothing items, and other products, restricting the amounts that consumers could purchase. All types of meats were rationed, as were cheeses, butter, and cooking oils. The government also urged American families to plant Victory gardens in their backyards. With Americans growing some of their own food at home, more food from farms could be shipped to soldiers at army bases and on battlefields.

In the twenty-first century, the group Food Not Lawns also encourages backyard food growing. The group notes that Americans burn more than 800 million gallons (3 billion liters) of fuel each year to power lawnmowers and that many homeowners also dowse their lawns with toxic chemical fertilizers and pesticides. Food Not Lawns argues that this land (totaling more than 40 million acres [16 million hectares] in the United States) would be much better utilized for growing organic vegetables to feed families.

During World War II, the US government encouraged Americans to plant Victory gardens at home. The gardens gave civilians more produce at a time when food purchases were rationed. And with civilians growing their own food, more farm-raised food could be shipped to soldiers.

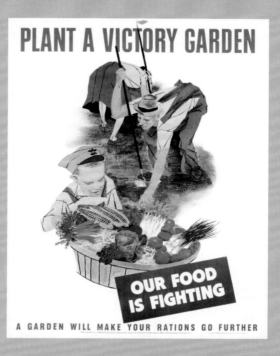

PLANT A VICTORY GARDEN

OUR FOOD IS FIGHTING

A GARDEN WILL MAKE YOUR RATIONS GO FURTHER

Macrobiotics, a diet heavily laden with organic brown rice, beans, and Asian sea vegetables, was one of the most visible hippie diets of the 1960s. The diet was devised by Sagen Ishizuka, a Japanese army doctor, at the close of the nineteenth century, as a way to improve his own health. In the mid-twentieth century, Japanese writer George Ohsawa promoted the diet around the world.

A vegetarian pioneer of this era was cookbook author and restaurateur Mollie Katzen, who helped start Moosewood Restaurant in Ithaca, New York, in the 1970s. Katzen is credited with "moving plant-based cuisine from the fringe to the center of the American dinner plate," according to *Organic Connections* magazine. Her classic *Moosewood Cookbook*, first published in 1974, offered a range of easy vegetarian recipes for the home cook. The recipes were based on what she and her staff prepared and served at the restaurant in Ithaca. The cookbook is still in print. A fortieth-anniversary edition came out in 2014.

Frances Moore Lappé, whose book *Diet for a Small Planet* came out in 1971, was among the first to reveal the inequalities of world food production. In addition to providing recipes and dietary information, she wrote about how millions of people around the world went hungry. At the same time, grains were raised with industrial farming practices that harmed the environment to feed cattle and other animals for meat and to feed people in wealthy nations. Many young Americans of this era were also influenced by Peter Singer's 1975 book *Animal Liberation*. Singer, an Australian, revealed the hideous cruelty inflicted on animals in factory farms. A moral philosopher, atheist, and professor, Singer wrote,

> From an ethical point of view, we all stand on an equal footing—whether we stand on two feet, or four, or none at all. The animal liberation movement is . . . saying that where animals and humans have similar interests—we might take the interest in avoiding physical pain as an example, for it is an interest that humans clearly share with other animals—those interests are to be counted equally, with no automatic discount just because one of the beings is

not human. A simple point, no doubt, but nevertheless part of a far-reaching ethical revolution.

In the late twentieth century, more and more Americans began to seek out vegetarian, organic, and locally grown foods. Farmers' markets, natural foods grocery stores, and vegetarian restaurants sprang up in many cities. In the 1990s, Alice Waters, owner of the famous, locally sourced Chez Panisse restaurant in Berkeley, California, launched the Edible Schoolyard project. The program and others like it have influenced educators across the United States to teach kids how to tend their own gardens and to cook nutritious lunches for themselves and their classmates.

In 2009 First Lady Michelle Obama planted an organic vegetable garden on the grounds of the White House. The garden provides fresh

First Lady Michelle Obama used the White House organic garden as a teaching tool. Here, the First Lady and visiting schoolchildren plant seedlings in the garden.

vegetables to the White House kitchen and also serves as an educational center for school groups that want to learn more about gardening. Through her gardening and educational activities, the First Lady promotes home gardening; school gardens; farmers' markets; exercise; and healthy, vegetable-heavy eating at home and at school.

CONTEMPORARY VEGGIES

In the twenty-first century, many people flirt with vegetarianism, fewer with veganism. Former US president Bill Clinton, having enjoyed fast food throughout much of his life, turned to a vegan diet after undergoing surgery for heart disease in 2010. But these days, he sounds more like a flexatarian. At his doctor's suggestion, he does eat fish and eggs, along with plants.

NO MEAT ON MONDAYS

The Meatless Monday movement encourages people to give up meat one day a week. Its origins date to World War I, when US civilians were asked to skip meat on Mondays so that more meat could be sent to soldiers and hungry civilians in Europe. The concept was relaunched in 2003 with support from the Center for a Livable Future at Johns Hopkins Bloomberg School of Public Health in Baltimore, Maryland.

Others around the world have joined the campaign. Meatless Monday asserts on its website that people in thirty-six countries are involved. Musician Paul McCartney of the Beatles and his daughter clothing designer Stella McCartney created a similar Meat Free Monday campaign in 2009. Paul wrote a song to spur the idea on. His group's slogan is "One day a week can make a world of difference." A similar group called reducetarians, an official online community, tries to help the planet by pledging to eat less meat for thirty days at a time.

Jay Z and Beyoncé promote veganism through a meal delivery service called 22 Days Nutrition. The world-famous entertainers have moved toward a plant-based diet, but they are not entirely vegan.

Actor Anne Hathaway, a longtime vegan, discovered while making the film *Interstellar* (2014) that her energy level was inadequate on, as she put it, "garbanzo beans on a plate." So she abandoned the vegan diet in favor of a high-protein paleo-style diet.

Part-time vegans Beyoncé and her husband, Jay Z, are partners in 22 Days Nutrition, a vegan meal delivery service based in Miami, Florida. Each meal is delivered ready to eat, and service is available across the continental United States. Created by chefs from organic veggies, meals cost fifteen dollars a pop.

British primatologist Jane Goodall, known for her studies of chimpanzees, is also a vegetarian. She read about factory farming and came to believe that a piece of meat stands for "fear, pain and death."

3 WHAT IS HEALTHY?

THE THREE MAIN CLASSES OF FOOD that provide energy to the body are proteins, carbohydrates, and fats. Made up of amino acids, the so-called building blocks of life, protein is found in the animals we eat. It is also found in dairy products, eggs, nuts, beans, potatoes, and sweet potatoes. Some fruits and green veggies, such as avocados and broccoli, also provide protein. Most North Americans get plenty of protein, but many people on Earth, especially children in sub-Saharan Africa and in parts of India, Pakistan, and Bangladesh, do not. They are poor, and their families cannot afford to buy high-protein foods.

Carbohydrates are chemical compounds formed by green plants. Nutritionists divide carbohydrates into two groups: simple and complex. Simple carbs are sweeteners such as table sugar (from corn or beets), honey (from bees), and corn syrup (from corn). Simple carbs provide a quick burst of energy. Complex carbs contain fiber, and the human body digests them more slowly. They come from veggies such as carrots and potatoes; from some fruits, such as apples and strawberries; and from beans, whole wheat, brown rice, and fresh corn. All carbs become sugars for your body to use. Unused sugars are turned into fat and stored in the body. Yes, carbs, not fats, can make you fat.

Fats insulate your body, keep your brain working well, give you energy, and help rebuild cells. They also feel good in the mouth and contribute to a feeling of satiety, or fullness. Journalists and others write about "good" versus "bad" fats, and it can be tough to know which is which. Butter was

WHAT ISN'T?

considered a valuable nutrient for millennia. But in the late twentieth century, as part of a campaign against fats, some nutritionists began to say that butter was bad. In the twenty-first century, nutritionists are again saying that butter is good—because it's derived from cows' milk and is not created through chemical processing. Vegetable oils, such as corn, soy, and peanut oil, once thought of as good, can be bad for you because they are highly processed using harmful chemicals. Trans-unsaturated fats (trans fats), made from vegetable oil and found in margarine and many processed foods, are definitely bad. These fats are thought to lead to heart disease,

FAT IN A CAN

Crisco, a hardened cottonseed oil intended to replace butter or lard, was introduced to US consumers in 1911. It was the first trans fat on the American market. Commercial bakers embraced it, as did home bakers, influenced by ads suggesting that Crisco was a better and more modern product than sorry old butter. Other trans fats on the US market of the twenty-first century include margarine, a cheap substitute for butter.

In the twenty-first century, with trans fats getting more and more bad publicity, Americans appear to be turning away from margarine. According to the *Wall Street Journal*, US sales of margarine have fallen dramatically since the mid-1990s, with sales of butter making a slow but steady climb upward. Meanwhile, the J. M. Smucker Company, which sells Crisco, has reformulated its product to remove all the trans fat.

cancer, stroke, and diabetes. Yet for decades, they have been commonly used in fast foods and other prepared foods. Manufacturers like them because they are inexpensive and have a long shelf life—that is, foods made with trans fats can sit on store shelves for months or even years without spoiling. In June 2015, the US Food and Drug Administration (FDA) officially issued a phase-out ban on trans fats in the US food industry. The agency gave the food industry three years to cease using trans fats—although companies can still use trans fats in products if they file a petition and win approval from the FDA. Some restaurant chains such as McDonald's and Chick-fil-A have already stopped frying foods with trans fats.

CUTTING THE FAT

Since the early 1970s, scientific studies have led Americans to believe that they should eat low-fat foods and veggies, avoid meats, and exercise more. Some scientists have said that saturated fats, which come from animal products, are linked to heart disease. Conventional wisdom also claims that fat people are fat because they eat too much fat. Right? Wrong.

Fat satisfies and, in moderate amounts, is good for the human body. However, beginning in the 1970s—as a result of a push from the US government, the American Heart Association, the American Diabetes Association, and other organizations—Americans began to cut back on fats. Many people replaced the fats with an increased intake of filling carbohydrates such as crackers, cookies, cereals, rice, and pasta. Seeing an opportunity to profit, many manufacturers removed fat from processed foods so they could advertise them as fat-free. But to satisfy consumers, who craved the "mouth feel" and fullness that comes from eating fats, manufacturers added more sugar and salt to products instead. People bought fat-free yet sugar- and sodium-heavy muffins and cookies, thinking that they were healthy options.

The American Heart Association pushed an unproven connection between fat intake and heart disease. Soon fats were said to be evil and

Some consumers think that foods labeled "fat-free" or "reduced fat" are healthy choices. But such products are often full of fattening carbohydrates.

carbohydrates were viewed as good. Carbs in moderation can be okay—as long as they come from veggies, fruits, and whole grains. But Americans began to get more and more carbs from tasty yet high-calorie, sugar-filled snacks and cereals rather than from nutritionally rich food sources. This trend, along with an increasingly sedentary lifestyle, led to an increase in obesity in the United States.

In 1980 the US Department of Agriculture (USDA) issued new federal dietary guidelines recommending a low-fat diet. Reissued every five years, the guidelines are the basis of all federal government food programs, such as school breakfast and lunch programs, food assistance for needy mothers and children, and other food assistance initiatives. The government's push toward a low-fat diet was backed by major growers and processors of vegetable oils, such as corn oil and soy oil. They saw a clear business opportunity as Americans turned away from butter (fat from cows) and lard (fat derived from pigs). Manufacturers claimed that vegetable oils were healthier than animal fats. They were also cheaper for the consumer.

Looking back on the low-fat frenzy of the late twentieth century, National Public Radio's Allison Aubrey reported in 2014, "The food industry saw the low-fat, high-carb mantra as an opportunity to create a whole new range of products. Fat-free frozen yogurt, fat-free muffins and cookies—the formula was: Take out the fat; add lots of sugar. By the early

'90s, foods with little or no fat were flying off the shelves. Pretzels were good (no fat); nuts were bad (loaded with fat). Baked potatoes were OK, but hold the sour cream. And salads? Sure, greens are great, but no oily salad dressing."

BIG FAT LIES

Journalist Nina Teicholz, whose book *The Big Fat Surprise: Why Butter, Meat and Cheese Belong in a Healthy Diet* came out in 2014, spent nine years investigating the push toward a low-fat diet for good health. She found the scientific arguments against fat to be unsubstantiated. "Almost nothing that we commonly believe about fats generally and saturated fat in particular appears, upon close examination, to be accurate," she writes.

Teicholz points to the Women's Health Initiative, a 1991 National Institutes of Health study of cardiovascular disease, cancer, and osteoporosis in women. The study monitored the health of forty-nine thousand American women for eight to twelve years. During the trial, participants cut back on meat and fat and increased their intake of vegetables, fruit, and whole grains. Teicholz writes, "These women not only failed to lose weight, but they also did not see any significant reduction in their risk for either heart disease or cancer of any major kind."

Teicholz says that while cutting back on fats, Americans of the twenty-first century are eating many more carbohydrates, "at least 25% more since the early 1970s." She also notes:

> Consumption of saturated fat, meanwhile, has dropped by 11%, according to the best available government data. Translation: Instead of meat, eggs and cheese, we're eating more pasta, grains, fruit and starchy vegetables such as potatoes. Even seemingly healthy low-fat foods, such as yogurt, are stealth carb-delivery systems, since removing the fat often requires the addition of fillers to make up for lost texture—and these [fillers] are usually carbohydrate-based.

THE FRENCH CHEF

Julia Child was the first television cooking star in the United States. In the 1960s, she taught Americans the secrets of French cuisine through her book *Mastering the Art of French Cooking* and via her TV show, *The French Chef.* In the late 1980s, according to biographer Bob Spitz, Child was astonished to learn that allegedly informed diet professionals were demonizing traditional ways of eating. Suddenly, "butter, cream, veal, sugar, marrow, potatoes and fat" had become "the seven dirty words you can't say on television" Child lamented. At the same time, newly absent from a discussion on eating was the concept of moderation. "Small helpings. Sample a little bit of everything. These are the secrets of happiness and good health. You need to enjoy the good things in life, but you need not overindulge," said Child. Child, who died at the age of ninety-one in 2004, was also quoted as saying, "I'm awfully sorry for people who are taken in by all of today's dietary mumbo jumbo. They are not getting any enjoyment out of their food."

Julia Child *(above)*, who taught French cooking to Americans with her 1960s TV cooking show and with her best-selling cookbooks, argued that the key to healthy eating lies in moderation.

Teicholz stresses that carbs can make you fat and that being overweight can lead to a condition called Type 2 diabetes. Type 2 diabetes, which occurs most often in middle-aged and elderly adults, develops when the body doesn't produce enough insulin and doesn't process it properly. Without insulin, the body cannot process glucose (a type of sugar), which then builds up in the bloodstream. If left untreated, diabetes can cause health problems such as blindness, kidney failure, heart attack, and stroke.

Gary Taubes, a journalist with an academic background in physics and engineering, wrote a 2007 book called *Good Calories, Bad Calories*. It explained how an unproven hypothesis about the health risks of eating meat and fat became dogma, perpetuated by those who determine US dietary policy. He blames refined carbohydrates for heart disease, diabetes, obesity, cancer, and other illnesses. In *Good Calories, Bad Calories,* he writes that "dietary fat, whether saturated or not, is not a cause of obesity, heart disease, or any other chronic disease of civilization."

Dr. Andrew Weil, founder and director of the Arizona Center for Integrative Medicine and a best-selling author on health and wellness, wrote this in 2010 on the topic of saturated fat:

> In my home state of Arizona, a restaurant named "Heart Attack Grill" does brisk business in Chandler, a Phoenix suburb. But the Grill's essential, in-your-face concept is that the saturated fat in beef clogs arteries, and hamburger meat is consequently among the most heart-damaging foods a human being can consume. . . . The problem? It's not true. The saturated fat lauded in this menu won't kill you. It may even be the safest element of the meal.

New York Times journalist Martha Rose Shulman, an influential food and recipe writer with more than twenty cookbooks to her name, has long promoted low-fat cooking. But in 2011, Shulman announced on her blog that she'd taken a "no more low-fat pledge." She wrote, "I took a pledge the other day that will surprise my longtime followers. It even surprised me. I pledged to drop the term 'low-fat' from my vocabulary." She also noted, "There are many recipes in my cookbooks from the '90s that now look and taste dated to me. I've put back some of the oil and cheese that I took out when editors were telling me to keep total fat at 30 percent of total calories—a concept that is now obsolete even among policymakers."

Few nutritionists will admit that they were wrong about the low-fat diet. But Tim Noakes, a professor of sports sciences at the University of Cape Town in South Africa, has done so. Noakes once taught that "carbo-loading" was imperative for athletes. He said that long-distance runners should eat big bowls of pasta a few nights in a row just before a race, so that they would have enough energy to compete. In the 2010s, Noakes promotes "fat-loading" instead. He says that athletes should eat a diet of butter, cream, coconut oil, vegetables, eggs, and healthily raised meats—he favors fatty lamb—before competing.

Another longtime low-fat fan who has changed views is Alice Lichtenstein, a professor of nutrition science and policy at Tufts University in Massachusetts and vice chair of the 2015 Dietary Guidelines Advisory Committee, which advises the USDA and the US Department of Health and Human Services. In September 2014, she was quoted in the *Wall Street Journal* as saying that low-fat diets were "probably not a good idea." In response, Nina Teicholz wrote, "It was a rare public acknowledgment

In the late twentieth century, some nutritionists advised long-distance runners to load up on carbohydrates the night before racing. The carbs were supposed to give runners extra energy. Many contemporary nutritionists disagree. They say that fats are better fuel for our bodies than are carbohydrates.

conceding the failure of the basic principle behind 35 years of official American nutrition advice." Whether or not the USDA's 2015 guidelines will reverse the government's low-fat stance is unknown.

PUSHBACK

Not everyone agrees that fat—especially animal fat—is okay. Dr. Neal Barnard, founder of the Physicians Committee for Responsible Medicine, advocates for an extremely low-fat, vegetable, and whole-grain-rich path. But he advises vegans and vegetarians to take vitamin B12, a substance that not only maintains healthy nerves and blood cells but also is involved in creating DNA, which carries our genetic material. B12 is commonly found in all animal foods, though not in plants. Barnard's fellow travelers on this plant-based path include American physicians Dean Ornish, Caldwell Esselstyn, and Joel Fuhrman and Professor T. Colin Campbell.

In the 1980s, Campbell examined the health of sixty-five hundred adults in China, where the typical diet is heavy on plants and low on meat. In their 2005 book *The China Study*, Campbell and his coauthor, his son Thomas, state, "The findings from the China Study indicate that the lower the percentage of animal-based foods that are consumed, the greater the health benefits—even when that percentage declines from 10 percent to 0 percent of calories." The Campbells suggested that an animal-free diet could help prevent cancer and Alzheimer's disease. But the study has taken fire from critics, who say that its findings are based on anecdotal evidence and not on hard data derived from strict clinical trials.

The 2011 documentary film *Forks over Knives*, based in part on the Campbells' work, also states that many diseases could be reversed or prevented if people would reject animal-based and processed foods and pursue a plant-based diet. Three years later, The *Forks over Knives Plan*, a 2014 book by Alona Pulde and Matthew Lederman, repeats the same "whole-food, plant-based diet" mantra. Whole food here means minimally processed foods, such as brown breads and rice still containing its hull. The authors encourage the exclusion of fatty animal products, including eggs, dairy, and butter.

Denise Minger is a health writer and lecturer with a reputation for aggressively challenging conventional wisdom. A former vegan from Portland, Oregon, she is the author of a 2014 book titled *Death by Food Pyramid: How Shoddy Science, Sketchy Politics and Shady Special Interests Have Ruined Our Health*. On her blog, *Raw Food SOS*, she challenges both the China Study and the *Forks over Knives* documentary, attacking the data as flawed. On his blog *Fat Head*, health writer Tom Naughton relates that Minger "shreds several of Campbell's leaps in logic, and uses his own data to show that some of the healthiest people in China live in regions with the highest levels of meat consumption."

THE MIDDLE WAY

While few experts refute that a largely plant-based diet is a solid approach to healthy eating, many find rigid veganism to be too extreme. Even the website Vegan.com, which is dedicated to promoting veganism, acknowledges, "The health advantages of a vegan diet aren't as pronounced as many animal advocates contend, and it's certainly possible to eat an extremely healthful diet that contains some animal products. That said, a vegan diet will automatically eliminate many of the most unhealthful foods that people regularly eat: hamburgers, hot dogs, sausages, fried chicken, ice cream, and so forth."

Many food writers and nutritionists agree that a healthy diet does not require avoiding all fat and animal products. They argue instead that people should reject heavily processed and refined commercial

NUTRITIONISTS NOTE THAT THE POOREST OF AMERICANS HAVE THE HIGHEST LEVELS OF OBESITY, HEART DISEASE, AND DIABETES—AND MANY OF THESE HEALTH PROBLEMS CAN BE RELATED TO A HIGH INTAKE OF PROCESSED FOODS.

The USDA's MyPlate program, released in 2011 as an alternative to the food pyramid, was designed to help Americans eat a range of foods. According to the USDA, fruits and vegetables should fill half your plate at each meal, with grains and protein taking up the rest. MyPlate recommends eating whole grains, such as whole wheat, oatmeal, or brown rice. It also advises choosing meats, poultry, seafood, beans and peas, nuts and seeds, and dairy products for protein.

food products. Nutritionists note that the poorest of Americans have the highest levels of obesity, heart disease, and diabetes—and many of these health problems can be related to a high intake of processed foods. It's junk food—frequently containing refined flours, sugar, and vegetable oils—that's causing the problem, not the fats in burgers, ribs, or chicken. By eliminating junk food from the diet and replacing it with fresh fruits, vegetables, whole grains, and lean meats, people are much more likely to lose weight and feel better. As nutritionist Kris Gunnars writes on his website Authority Nutrition, "I personally find it plausible that the benefits of vegan diets are largely caused by avoiding processed foods and harmful ingredients like added sugar. It has absolutely nothing to do with avoiding unprocessed animal foods."

Meat and veggie lover Mark Bittman, author, food guru for the *New York Times*, and a regular diner-out, created a unique solution for his own weight problem after his doctor told him that he was 40 pounds (18 kg) overweight and prediabetic. Bittman's idea was to eat vegan every day, all day, right up until dinnertime. At dinner he let himself eat anything he wanted, including meats and cheese. He knew that dinner was a social meal, often enjoyed with friends. For this reason, he felt that it would be much easier to pursue a vegan diet morning and noon, when he was less likely to be eating with other people, than to put limits on the evening dining menu. In the first month of trying out his notion, he lost 15 pounds (6.8 kg). In 2013 he wrote a book called *VB6: Eat Vegan before 6:00* about his pursuit. He lost 36 pounds (16 kg) during the writing of the book.

Dr. Georgia Ede, a physician and psychiatrist who works at Smith College in Northampton, Massachusetts, took a deep look at diet to solve her own health problems. She notes the complexities of dietary behavior, writing on her website, Diagnosis: Diet:

> Because people believe vegetables are healthy, people who eat more vegetables tend to be more health-conscious in general. However, health-conscious people also tend to do lots of other things differently from the average person—they may eat less processed food, drink less alcohol, smoke less, eat less sugar, count calories, exercise more, etc. These other differences are very hard to account for in studies. The only way to really figure out if vegetables are healthy is to compare a diet with vegetables to a diet without vegetables. I know of no scientific study that has done this.

MORE MALIGNED FOODS
GLUTEN

Gluten-free diets have fully engaged the attention of the American public since the early twenty-first century. Gluten is a combination of proteins found in certain grains (including wheat, rye, and barley). Gluten is the ingredient that makes dough from these grains sticky and elastic. (The words *glue* and *gluten* both come from a Latin word meaning "clay.")

People who suffer from celiac disease, an autoimmune ailment, must avoid gluten, which can damage their intestines and make them sick. Only about 1 percent of the US public has celiac disease. But many other people are gluten-sensitive—they may find that their stomachs bloat after eating

Wheat is harvested on a large industrial farm on the Great Plains. Used to make bread, pasta, and many other foods, wheat is a staple of the American diet. Some argue that gluten from wheat and other grains is unhealthy, but the scientific arguments for a gluten-free diet are slim.

a bowl of white-flour pasta, for instance. Many people believe that wheat gluten in particular can cause weight gain, put people at risk for heart disease and diabetes, and create troublesome intestinal reactions.

Some scientists say that gluten is harmful to the body because it's relatively new to the human diet—and therefore our digestive system has not yet adapted to process it. Real Meal Revolution (the companion website to *The Real Meal Revolution*, a book Tim Noakes wrote in 2015 with a chef and a nutritionist) states that meats, veggies, and fruits have been human staples for millions of years. Grains and gluten, on the other hand, introduced only with the development of agriculture about twelve thousand years ago, are comparatively new in the human diet. Noakes writes, "If you could put the entire human history into one day, we have only been eating cereals and grains for five minutes . . . a very short amount of time in our existence."

Other experts think that the quick-acting yeast used in both commercial and home bread making (compared to slower-rising yeast-based products such as sourdough) has made many wheat breads less digestible and has led to gluten sensitivity. Barbara Griggs, writing in the British newspaper the *Guardian*, explains, "In the long slow fermentation that produces sourdough bread, important nutrients such as iron, zinc and magnesium, antioxidants, folic acid, and other B vitamins become easier for our bodies to absorb." In other words, these nutrients are predigested during fermentation. And also during the fermentation process, "gluten is broken down and rendered virtually harmless." In effect, the sourdough starter "eats" the gluten—so we don't have to.

Many Americans assume that gluten-free foods offer health benefits, and they choose a gluten-free diet without first seeking input from a medical professional. In fact, scientists say that the evidence for the benefits of a gluten-free diet is slim—except for those who have been diagnosed with celiac disease. Nevertheless, the gluten-free food market is booming, with the US market expected to hit $24 billion in sales per year by 2020.

In some ways, gluten-free foods are not all they're cracked up to be. For one thing, gluten-free foods such as English muffins and pancake mixes tend to be high in carbohydrates such as rice starch, cornstarch, tapioca starch, and potato starch. And they are sometimes filled with ingredients on the junk list, including guar gum, artificial flavorings, dyes, and chemical preservatives. In addition, these products are usually more costly than what they aim to replace. Finally, many foods that don't contain gluten in the first place are now being labeled "gluten-free." Hummus—that chickpea and tahini dip beloved by snackers—is one of them. Why the label? Simply put, it makes for more sales.

CHOLESTEROL

Cholesterol is another substance that has a lousy reputation. But it can be good or bad, depending on its chemical makeup. Cholesterol is a fatty substance made by the liver to keep cells working smoothly. It is important in digestion and the creation of hormones, as well as the production of vitamin D in the body. In addition to the cholesterol produced in the liver, cholesterol also enters our bodies from meat, egg yolks, butter, cheese, and some plants.

Doctors talk about "bad" cholesterol and "good" cholesterol. Low-density lipoprotein (LDL) is the bad kind of cholesterol. It is linked to heart disease. High-density lipoprotein (HDL) is good cholesterol that removes bad cholesterol from the bloodstream. The bad kind comes from trans fats, carbohydrates, and certain oils, such as soy, corn, peanut, and almond oil. Foods that boost good cholesterol include soy, nuts, and beans.

SUGAR

Increasingly, American consumers are recognizing that both sugar and corn syrup are unhealthy. Sales of soft drinks, most of which contain corn syrup, have declined steadily since the first decade of the twenty-first century, the tenth straight yearly decline. In 2014 the per capita consumption of carbonated soft drinks in the United States fell to its lowest level since 1986. Americans are buying bottled water instead, with 2014 sales up 7.3 percent over the year before.

Doctors generally agree that sugar is bad for you. Too much sugar can lead to tooth decay, obesity, and other health problems. When you drink an extra-large soda like the one shown here, you're taking in the equivalent of more than forty-eight packets of sugar.

Some soft drink companies have tried to convince consumers that soda made with sugar is less harmful than soda made with corn syrup, but nutritionists say there's really no difference. As business journalist Daniel Kline writes, "Real sugar soda may be the current version of low tar cigarettes [which are touted as safer than other cigarettes], [and] there is an audience that's not looking for actually healthy products just ones that sort of appear so. For those deluded folks Pepsi Made With Real Sugar should hit the spot."

Some states and cities have tried to discourage consumers from drinking sugary soft drinks by taxing the products heavily. In 2013 New York City tried to prohibit restaurants from selling supersized sugary drinks (more than 16 ounces [0.5 liters]), but the state's supreme court struck down the ban. Such efforts also come up against the giant soft drink producers, who have the megabucks to fight such initiatives. "The American Beverage Association—Coca-Cola and Pepsi Cola—are pouring millions and millions of dollars into making sure that no state or locality passes a soda tax. Or that nobody says anything bad about sodas. I mean, they're really hard at work at that," observes nutritionist and author Marion Nestle.

Dr. Robert Lustig, author of *Fat Chance: Beating the Odds against Sugar, Processed Food, Obesity, and Disease* (2012), concludes, "Sugar causes diseases: unrelated to their calories and unrelated to the attendant weight gain. It's an independent primary-risk factor. Now, there will be food-industry people who deny it until the day they die, because their livelihood depends on it."

> "REAL SUGAR SODA MAY BE THE CURRENT VERSION OF LOW TAR CIGARETTES."
>
> —Daniel Kline

4 DOWN ON

agriculture is big business, dominated by large industrial farms. The leaders of these corporate farms don't usually ask, "How can we best use this land to feed people?" Rather they ask, "What crops will bring our shareholders the biggest profit?" This quest for profits has led to great inequalities. For instance, in many poor parts of the world, such as Africa and Southeast Asia, investment companies from the United States, Europe, and China have bought up vast tracts of land and created giant farms. The farms produce crops such as coffee, tea, cacao, and fruits, which are then sold to foreign purchasers for huge profits. Meanwhile, local peoples are often undernourished.

Experts say that farmers produce enough food to feed everyone on the planet, but this food is not being distributed fairly. And for many people, the food is not affordable. Even in a rich nation such as the United States, about 47 million people—or roughly 15 percent of the population—cannot afford to buy the food they need without help from government assistance programs.

BUSINESS AS USUAL

Modern corporate farms are run like factories. Whether they are raising crops or animals, corporate farmers try to maximize their outputs— and thus their profits—with the help of high-tech equipment, chemical pesticides and fertilizers, and economies of scale (reducing the cost of making a product by manufacturing or growing it in large quantities).

THE FARM

Monoculture, or growing the same type of crop on a piece of land year after year, is common on large industrial farms. This practice enables farmers to efficiently grow and harvest vast quantities of certain crops. Rather than having to tend to many different kinds of plants, each requiring different amounts of water, fertilizer, and pesticides—and each with a different planting and harvesting schedule—farmers can apply one system to the whole farm. Yet this approach to agriculture can deplete the soil of key nutrients because crops that are typically grown using monoculture, especially corn, draw large amounts of nitrogen from the soil.

To add nitrogen and other nutrients back to the soil, industrial farmers often apply chemical fertilizers. And to fight insects, diseases, and weeds, industrial farmers generally apply chemical pesticides to their fields. But during rainstorms, excess chemicals can wash off farm fields and end up in soil, groundwater, and nearby waterways. Chef and food writer Deborah Madison remarks, "Our soil in [the United States] is tired. It's been infused with pesticides, chemical fertilizers, synthetic nitrogen, along with incessant plowing, and the planting of monocultural crops. Its health has been neglected in favor of relentless production."

When raising food animals, industrial farmers also try to maximize efficiency. At animal feedlots, cattle, pigs, chickens, and other livestock are crowded together in pens and cages. To quickly fatten livestock for slaughter, workers inject animals with growth hormones and add

Animal welfare activists decry the treatment of livestock on large factory farms, like this one in Bloomfield, Nebraska. At the typical industrial farm, animals are crowded into stalls and cages, with no room to move freely.

antibiotics (which are normally used to fight infectious diseases) to the food, even for healthy animals.

On industrial farms, every aspect of raising livestock—from birth to feeding to slaughter—is mechanized. For instance, when chickens are ready to be slaughtered, workers hang them upside down, with their feet attached to conveyer belts. Then the workers dunk twenty birds at a time into a saltwater bath called a stun cabinet for seven seconds. A mild electric current running through the water paralyses the birds, whose necks are then cut by rotating blades. *New York Times* food writer Mark Bittman notes that the US chicken industry kills more than six hundred thousand birds this way every single hour of every single day. In 2015 he wrote, "Almost all of those birds are raised in conditions that range from unnatural to torturous."

The handling and slaughter of larger animals can be even more gruesome. At meat processing plants, animals are often dragged from trucks and sometimes beaten as they are led to the slaughter. Before killing pigs, workers use an electric current to render them unconscious and then cut their throats. Cows are stunned before slaughter with a shot to the head from a metal bolt. Workers who do the slaughtering on industrial chicken farms or in huge pig or cattle processing plants don't stay long in these jobs. The work is relentlessly repetitive, depressing, dirty, and dangerous.

BIG CORN

The US government supports large farms with tax breaks and other financial aid known as subsidies. Such programs were originally designed to keep food prices low or stable, to keep farm businesses financially healthy, and to ensure a plentiful food supply for Americans. But critics say that in the twenty-first century, farm subsidies aren't given out fairly and that they no longer are used to ensure that US consumers have access to healthy and inexpensive food.

Critics note that the corn industry receives billions of dollars in farm subsidies each year, even though most of the corn grown in the United States is not used to feed Americans. Instead, the bulk of US-grown corn is either exported, made into ethanol (fuel made from plants), or fed to animals. A small percentage is turned into high-fructose corn syrup for soft drinks. Only about 1 percent of all corn grown in the United States ends up on your summer dinner plate, in the form of cobs dripping with butter. Writer Eric Pianin of the *Fiscal Times* provides some numbers: "Of the $277 billion spent on farm subsidy programs since 1995, about $81.7 billion went to subsidize corn," as compared to "$637 million for apples or vegetables," he writes.

Pianin and others decry giving tax breaks to corn growers, whose products, including corn syrup, corn starch, and vegetable shortening, contribute to obesity, diabetes, and other health problems. In 2013, in a report published in *Scientific American*, journalist Jonathan Foley suggested that "diversifying the Corn Belt [the corn-growing region of the midwestern United States] into a wider mix of agricultural systems, including other crops and grass-fed animal operations, could produce substantially more food—and a more diverse and nutritious diet—than the current system."

GENETIC ENGINEERING

Ever since humans started planting seeds, raising livestock, and living in settled communities, farmers have been modifying crops and animals. For instance, early farmers would choose the most nutritious grain varieties and replant only those types, mate the wooliest sheep with one another, graft different fruit tree varieties together to produce sweeter fruits, and breed only those peas that were not susceptible to mold.

In the twenty-first century, farmers still modify plants and animals, but they often do so using genetic engineering. Genetic engineers are lab scientists who alter the makeup of plant or animal genes—the biochemical markers that determine the characteristics of living things—to introduce certain desirable traits. For instance, fruits might be genetically engineered for increased shelf life or better taste. Pigs and other livestock might

GOOD BREEDING

The historical breeding of plants of the species *Brassica oleracea* (which includes the unexciting cabbage plant) has given us a diverse range of green vegetables. By selectively breeding desirable plants of this species, farmers have created broccoli, broccolini, brussels sprouts, cauliflower, kale, and collard greens, to name just a few. Broccoli, for example, was developed by Italian growers as early as the sixteenth century. In the late nineteenth century, Thomas Jefferson imported broccoli seeds from Italy to plant in his own garden at Monticello in Virginia. Broccolini, created by crossbreeding Chinese green gai lan and broccoli, has been available since the late 1990s. Kalettes, or kale sprouts, are the new kids on the *Brassica oleracea* block. The plant is a kale/brussels sprouts combo that made a slow debut in the United Kingdom in 2010 and is creeping into US stores.

Big Corn dominates US agriculture. Much of the US corn crop is made into ethanol, corn syrup, and animal feed. Cornfields are often heavily treated with pesticides and synthetic fertilizers.

be engineered to produce less fatty meat. Many food crops have been engineered to tolerate herbicides. With herbicide-resistant crops, farmers can spray large amounts of weed killer on their fields knowing that only the weeds will die, not the crops.

By 2013 growers were raising herbicide-resistant soy, corn, and cotton on 169 million acres (68 million hectares) of farmland in the United States. The USDA elaborates on this:

> Genetically engineered (GE) varieties with pest management traits became commercially available for major crops in 1996. More than 15 years later, adoption of these varieties by U.S. farmers is widespread and U.S. consumers eat many products derived from GE crops—including cornmeal, oils, and sugars—largely unaware that these products were derived from GE crops.

Many consumers are wary of genetically modified organisms (GMOs), however. They worry that foods derived from them are not safe to eat. They especially worry that herbicide-resistant plants might be harmful, since the plants take up herbicides—which have been sprayed to kill the weeds around them—through their roots. David Schubert of the California-based Salk Institute for Biological Studies explains:

> Until the introduction of [GMOs] about 20 years ago [the mid-1990s], herbicides were sprayed on fields before planting, and then only sparingly used around crops. The food that we ate from the plants was free of these chemicals.
>
> In stark contrast, with herbicide resistant GM plants, the herbicides and a mixture of other chemicals (surfactants) required to get the active ingredient into the plant are sprayed directly on the crops and are then taken up into the plant. The surrounding weeds are killed while the GM plant is engineered to resist the herbicide. Therefore, the food crop itself contains the herbicide.

FRANKENFOODS

Genetic engineers are also hard at work modifying food animals. An example is "Frankensalmon," fishes that grow twice as fast and twice as big as typical salmon and can therefore be brought to market sooner. (The nicknames Frankenfoods, Frankensalmon, and so on come from Frankenstein's monster, an out-of-control being created by a scientist in Mary Shelley's 1818 book *Frankenstein*.)

A 2015 *New York Times* article revealed that at one government research facility in Nebraska, "scientists are using surgery and breeding techniques to re-engineer [genetically modify] the farm animal to fit the needs of the 21st-century meat industry. The potential benefits are huge: animals that produce more offspring, yield more meat and cost less to raise." But as the article goes on to explain, such experiments have a dark side:

> Pigs are having many more piglets—up to 14, instead of the usual eight—but hundreds of those newborns, too frail or crowded to move, are being crushed each year when their mothers roll over. Cows, which normally bear one calf

at a time, have been retooled to have twins and triplets, which often emerge weakened or deformed, dying in such numbers that even meat producers have been repulsed.

This report horrified so many readers and was shared so thoroughly in social media that it galvanized thousands of people to write, call, and corner their representatives in the US Congress. The result was that within three weeks of the publication of the report in the *New York Times*, a bipartisan group in both houses of Congress introduced a bill requiring that the federal Animal Welfare Act (AWA) be updated. Passed in 1966, the AWA calls for the humane treatment of animals during exhibition, transportation, sale, and medical research, but it does not apply to animals used in agricultural research at government facilities. If the 2015 bill passes into law, such animals would be protected from inhumane treatment. Meanwhile, the bill has been sent to a congressional committee for further study.

US food manufacturers are not required to label foods to indicate that they have been genetically engineered or that they contain GMO ingredients. So, millions of consumers are eating GMO foods without knowing it. Many consumer advocates argue that GMO foods are not safe. The Institute for Responsible Technology, a nonprofit policy organization based in Iowa, has noted instances of organ damage, reproductive problems, and other health problems in laboratory animals and farm animals fed GMO foods. Some studies link GMO foods to increased risks for cancer in humans.

Activists say that GMO products should be labeled as such, so that consumers can avoid them if they choose. The food industry opposes labeling, arguing that GMO foods are safe and that labels would send the message that they aren't. The FDA asserts that GMO foods are safe to eat, although many nations—including Australia, China, France, Germany, Greece, India, Mexico, and Russia—have banned some or all GMOs, and many more nations require GMO labeling. In July 2015, a bill that would prevent US states from requiring labeling (Vermont, Maine, and

Connecticut have enacted such requirements) passed in the US House of Representatives. The next step for the bill is passage in the US Senate. If it passes there, it goes to the president for approval.

HOT AND DRY

Planet Earth is facing a crisis, and industrial agriculture is part of the problem. The burning of fossil fuels—petroleum, coal, and natural gas—for manufacturing, home heating and power, agriculture, and transportation puts excess carbon dioxide into the atmosphere. Carbon dioxide traps heat from the sun, leading to higher temperatures on Earth. Higher temperatures have in turn led to climate change—with more intense storms and flooding in some places and drought conditions in others.

Industrialized farms use heavy machinery—plows, tractors, harvesters, and other vehicles—that burn large amounts of fossils fuels, thus contributing to climate change. Furthermore, some of the nitrogen fertilizer used on industrial farms escapes into the atmosphere as nitrous oxide, a gas that has "nearly 300 times the heat-trapping power of carbon dioxide," according to *Mother Jones* magazine. Nitrous oxide fuels climate change even further. And food grown on industrial farms is typically transported to consumers hundreds and even thousands of miles away via trucks, trains, and ships—which also run on fossil fuels and thus exacerbate climate change.

As Earth experiences more drought, clean freshwater has become an increasingly scarce resource. Large, industrialized farms use enormous amounts of water. In the midwestern United States, most farmers apply water to the surface of the soil, either by overhead sprinkler systems or by flooding an entire field or individual rows of crops. Much of this water runs off the surface rather than soaking into the soil. With sprinkler systems, additional water is lost through evaporation before it even reaches the soil surface.

The world cannot afford to waste water because supplies are running dry. For instance, most midwestern farmers pump water for irrigation from the Ogallala Aquifer, a vast underground reservoir spreading beneath parts of South Dakota, Wyoming, Colorado, Nebraska, Kansas, Oklahoma, Texas, and New Mexico. In the 1950s, the average depth of water in the aquifer was 240 feet (73 meters). Since then cities and farms have pumped water from the aquifer faster than it has been replenished by natural sources, such as rainwater and snowmelt. By 2014 the average depth of the aquifer was only about 80 feet (24 m)—a drop of about two-thirds since the 1950s. Scientists say that if rates of depletion continue, the aquifer will run dry completely by 2040.

Increasingly, droughts are devastating agricultural regions around the globe. For instance, drought struck California—the heart of US fruit, nut, and vegetable farming—in the second decade of the twenty-first century. Without enough rain, California farmers have had to pump more groundwater to irrigate their crops. In some cases, crops have withered in the fields. Or farmers have simply let fields lie fallow (unplanted). Farm owners have had to lay off workers, since they aren't needed to harvest and process crops, and the layoffs hurt California's economy. As certain fruits, nuts, and vegetables have become scarcer, their

Climate change has led to increased droughts in many places on Earth. Without enough water, crops can't survive, and without crops, people go hungry. In this image, grapevines in the United Kingdom wither due to drought.

prices have risen. Some California ranches have had to sell off or slaughter farm animals, because water to clean the animals, keep them hydrated, and grow their food is in such short supply.

THE SUSTAINABILITY MOVEMENT

To continue providing the world with food, in the face of dwindling water supplies, farmers will have to make changes. For instance, rather than growing tomatoes, which require more than 1 gallon (3.8 liters) of water per plant per day, farmers might switch to growing vegetables, such as beans and melons, that don't require as much water. Some farmers have switched from water-wasting overhead sprinklers and flooding to drip irrigation systems, which apply water directly to the top of the soil or slightly beneath it. With drip irrigation, little water is lost to evaporation and runoff. Around the world, more farmers are using old-fashioned practices such as water harvesting, which involves capturing rainwater in cisterns and other receptacles and using it to irrigate crops. In places with seasonal rains, such as sub-Saharan Africa, farmers can capture water in the rainy season and save it until the dry season. In many places, farmers are turning to no-till methods—that is, choosing not to plow fields before planting or to remove stubble and roots from fields after the harvest. Instead, farmers plant seeds among the previous year's stubble and roots using devices called seed drills. This process increases the amount of organic matter in the soil. In turn, that organic matter traps much-needed water. It also traps fertilizer that otherwise might run off into nearby rivers and lakes. Such changes are part of a larger environmental movement called

> TO CONTINUE PROVIDING THE WORLD WITH FOOD, IN THE FACE OF DWINDLING WATER SUPPLIES, FARMERS WILL HAVE TO MAKE CHANGES.

sustainable agriculture—that is, farming methods that do not permanently damage the land or permanently deplete resources.

Sustainable farms incorporate a number of different practices. One is biodiversity. Biodiversity, or integrating three to four crops in rotation on a typical farm, is better for the soil than monoculture, especially if one crop in the rotation is a legume, such as beans or peas. Some crops, such as corn, take large amounts of nitrogen from the soil. Farmers must therefore apply large amounts of chemical fertilizer to fields to replace the nitrogen. Legumes, on the other hand, get their nitrogen from soil-dwelling bacteria that grow along with them. These bacteria take nitrogen gas from air in the soil and feed it to the growing legumes. After the legumes are harvested, their remaining roots and stocks are plowed back into the soil or used for compost. This plant material is nitrogen-rich and provides nourishment for the next season's crop. In this way, biodiversity helps keep the soil fertile. In addition, if a farmer plants several crops in a field and a certain insect or disease targets one kind of plant specifically, the other plants will still survive—ensuring that the farmer's entire crop doesn't get wiped out.

Some farmers also integrate livestock into biodiverse farms. Instead of using chemical fertilizers, they add manure from their animals to cropland. Manure is natural fertilizer, produced on the farm for free. Unlike artificial fertilizers, it does not introduce harmful chemicals into the soil or into food crops. (However, if manure is not managed carefully, it can still run off of fields and pollute lakes and rivers.) In addition, animals on biodiverse farms help keep the soil aerated, or filled with healthy oxygen, by churning up the ground with their hooves.

HAPPIER ANIMALS

On sustainable farms, cattle and other animals are allowed to graze in open fields of grasses. Grass is a natural food for cattle, so it doesn't distress their digestive systems the way corn and other grains do. It does not contain the harmful antibiotics and hormones that are commonly fed to animals on industrial farms. Doctors note that grass-fed beef is healthier to eat than

On sustainable farms, plants and animals benefit one another. Animals add manure—natural fertilizer—to the soil. They also mix in healthy oxygen by churning up the soil with their hooves. In turn, cover crops and grasses provide healthy food for grazing animals. On this sustainable farm in Georgia, cows graze on the pearl millet cover crop, while sorghum *(background)* is grown for grain.

corn-fed beef. Grass-fed beef contains less saturated fat and more healthy acids, vitamins, and other nutrients. Raising cattle this way is not without problems, however. It takes huge tracts of land and large amounts of water (whether from rain or irrigation) to raise grass-fed cattle. And according to *Cooking Light* magazine, a feedlot cow on an industrial farm grows to slaughter weight up to one year faster than a cow fed on grass. The extra time invested in raising grass-fed cattle translates into higher costs for the farmer—and these costs are passed on to consumers in the form of higher beef prices. But the animals are healthier than those raised in pens—and therefore their meat is healthier to eat. They also live freer, happier lives.

When they are ready for market, animals raised on sustainable farms are slaughtered using humane methods. Berlin Reed, who calls himself the ethical butcher, witnessed the slaughtering of a pig on a sustainable farm in California around 2010. He noted, "For a big animal like a pig, shooting is absolutely the quickest and least stressful way to go." He continued, "These pigs were seconds from their death and the air was calm. I watched

VEGAN TO BUTCHER

Formerly a vegan, Berlin Reed of Portland, Oregon, calls himself "the ethical butcher." He decided that being vegan—though it is a positive ethical and political choice—was not likely to change the way food is produced in the United States. So he left what he calls the Church of the Righteous Herbivore after deciding two things: first, that meat is a deeply cultural part of eating worldwide and, second, that his mission is to reform the way food animals are handled, raised, and killed—which he believes should be done swiftly and painlessly. He also realized that the way to create change and to chip away at the industrial food business was to buy from local farmers who raise healthy animals humanely.

Reed trained as a butcher, educated himself regarding animal food factories, and learned to cook. Then he started a blog and began traveling; hosting cooking events; and urging young people to advocate for fresh, locally sourced produce and meats. "Meat is not meant to be eaten several times a day, every day. It is meant to be a hard won prize," he wrote.

His 2013 book *The Ethical Butcher* explains his philosophy well: "What, why, and how we eat is shaping the planet and our future. Throw out the guilt trips, give up on the jargon, and look in the mirror. Real food is still out there for all of us, and it is up to all of us to take it back."

Mac [the rancher] raise his gun, point it squarely between the eyes of the first pig, and POP! The pig fell like a cardboard cutout."

Humane Farm Animal Care (HFAC), a nonprofit group based in Herndon, Virginia, awards seals of approval to farms that meet the group's requirements for the humane treatment of food animals. These requirements include not crowding animals in cages or stalls and not using antibiotics to fatten animals. But there is much work to be done. HFAC does not require that farms provide sun and outdoor pastureland for animals. In addition, HFAC supports the killing techniques used at commercial slaughterhouses, a stance that has earned the organization criticism from animal welfare groups such as Free from Harm.

A woman deeply sensitive to the needs of animals is Temple Grandin. With a doctorate in animal sciences from the University of Illinois, Grandin has developed widely used guidelines to make commercial slaughter less traumatic for cows, pigs, and sheep, while also ensuring better-quality meat. (Less-stressed animals produce more lactic acid, which makes their meat tastier and tenderer.) Grandin devised the curved corral, a long sloping entry into the killing area. Traditionally, animals are herded into the area in a straight line. The curved entryway is thought to be less frightening for the animals, reducing their stress before slaughter. Grandin also suggests the elimination of excess noise and harsh lighting in slaughterhouses and outlines the effective and humane use of electric prods, stunning equipment, and other tools for handling animals during their slaughter. Her guidelines, published by the American Meat Institute, serve as recommendations for commercial slaughterhouses across the United States.

Animals raised on cozy storybook farms with red barns are still greatly in the minority in the United States, but increasingly, animal farms are choosing to raise healthier, happier food animals. For example, for twenty-three years, Carole Morison and her husband, Frank, of Pocomoke City, Maryland, ran one of the dozens of industrial chicken-raising operations under contract with Perdue Farms, a mega processor of poultry. Carole Morison was featured in the 2009 documentary film *Food, Inc.* Wearing a face mask as she stood amid the dust and feather chaos of her broiler chicken operation, Morison displayed visible disgust at the cruelty of corporate chicken raising.

Unwilling to convert their small operation to a larger one requested by Perdue—with up to forty thousand birds crammed into windowless huts, ripe with foul odors and disease—the Morisons lost their Perdue contract. So in 2010, they gave up their broiler operation and started a free-range egg-producing farm on 14 acres (5.7 hectares), with five hundred hens. By 2015 they had more than twelve hundred happy hens, thriving on a diet of healthy grains. Chickens are omnivores. In the wild, they eat grasses, weeds, bugs, and worms. On commercial farms, chickens are often given low-quality food, containing antibiotics, pesticides, and animal by-products. Morison says that her "vegetarian" chickens are healthier than those raised on commercial chicken farms and that their eggs are tastier. But like many small businesspeople, Morison struggles to make her farm financially successful.

THE ORGANIC OPTION

Most of us don't research the chemicals in our food supply. But we do hear of the risks of eating pesticide- and herbicide-laden foods, and we don't like the sound of them. Seeking healthier food raised through green, Earth-friendly methods, many consumers choose food from organic farms. Organic farmers don't use synthetic pesticides or chemical fertilizers. Instead, they grow food in healthy, chemical-free soil. They plant a diverse range of crops and use low-tech methods of weed killing, sometimes even employing geese to pluck harmful insects from the plants.

While many organic growers operate small farms, some organic farms are giants. For instance, Earthbound Farm has more than 37,000 acres (15,000 hectares) planted in organic greens in the United States, New Zealand, Peru, Mexico, and elsewhere. The company supplies organic produce to big box stores such as Walmart and Costco. Anna Lappé, the daughter of Francis Moore Lappé, writes, "As of 2012, 162 countries reported acreage of [government-] certified organic farms covering 37.5 million hectares [92.7 million acres] worldwide, a significant undercount of the total since not all farmers are officially certified. Although the United States has the largest market for organic food, 80 percent of all organic producers farm in developing [poor] countries, with India, Uganda, Mexico, and Tanzania leading the pack."

Organic food is usually more expensive than food grown with conventional methods. But health-conscious consumers who can afford the extra cost think it's worth it. In 2014 sales of organic foods and other products (such as soaps and lotions) in the United States rose 11.3 percent over the previous year, with total sales hitting $39.1 billion.

Organic vegetables are more expensive than conventional ones for several reasons. Organic farming involves the use of organic fertilizers, which come from living materials such as compost and animal manure. They take longer to produce than fertilizers made from chemicals and are therefore more expensive. Plants grown organically attract more weeds, since organic growers do not use chemical herbicides. Organic farmers often hire people to remove weeds by hand—a costly and time-consuming process. To be certified in the United States as an organic farmer (the USDA oversees organic certification), a grower must fill out detailed paperwork, pay certification fees, and undergo yearly inspections. In addition, a farmer can't simply switch from growing conventionally to growing organically. Before organic certification, farmland must be chemical-free for three years—a lengthy delay that also can cut into profits. Organic products that are grown outside the United States are often shipped to US markets (and other nations), and this too costs money. In short, running an organic farm is likely to be more expensive than running a conventional, industrialized farm, and organic growers often pass on part of the costs to customers in the form of higher prices.

Some critics say that big organic farms aren't that much better than big industrial farms. In a globalized marketplace, organic farms ship their products worldwide using polluting fossil fuels, which add carbon dioxide into the air and contribute to climate change. "How friendly to the environment are bagged salad greens shipped 8,000 miles [12,875 km] from New Zealand or tomatoes grown in the Mexican desert?" asks writer Barry Yeoman in the *Saturday Evening Post*.

BUY LOCAL

For many people, a solution is to buy food from small local farms, which might not be entirely organic but which usually limit their use of chemical fertilizers. Buying locally also ensures that consumers get the most nutrients possible from the foods they buy, since plants deliver

"HOW FRIENDLY TO THE ENVIRONMENT ARE BAGGED SALAD GREENS SHIPPED 8,000 MILES [12,875 KM] FROM NEW ZEALAND OR TOMATOES GROWN IN THE MEXICAN DESERT?"

—Barry Yeoman

their full nutritional value when eaten fresh, less so when transported by refrigerated trucks across the country or by ship across the ocean. Experts say that greens stored in your fridge should be eaten within a few days. Nutritionist Cinda S. Chima elaborates: "Researchers at [Pennsylvania State University] recently studied the effects of storage on the nutrient content of fresh spinach. Spinach stored at cooler temperatures retained more nutrients than at warmer temperatures. But even at 39 degrees [Fahrenheit, or 3.9°C], the spinach retained only 53 percent of its folate [a necessary B vitamin] after eight days."

Small farms have some advantages in the marketplace, because they can operate without costly middlemen. They might deal directly with consumers via farmers' markets and community supported agriculture (CSA). In CSA programs, families and restaurants pay farmers upfront each season for a weekly delivery of fresh produce. But small-scale farming is only a tiny fraction of the modern agricultural marketplace, which is dominated by big producers.

CRICKETS, ANYONE? The Food and Agriculture Organization of the United Nations estimates that in the 2010s, two billion people in the world are eating insects regularly. Insects are high in protein, and harvesting them for food takes much less energy than raising animals in feedlots. "Today, 80% of the world still eats over 1,600 species of insects," wrote fitness blogger Mark Sisson in 2013 "from Jing Leed [crickets] in Thailand to Escamoles [ant larvae] in Mexico to Casu Marzu [sheep milk cheese made with fly larvae] in Italy."

In 2013 two students at Brown University in Rhode Island decided to create protein-rich, non-carb flour from crickets. They started with an oven to roast the insects and a blender to grind them into a fine flour. Then they opened a company called Exo, based in New York City. Exo sells energy bars made with cricket flour.

But will Americans and Europeans take the bug bite? History shows that food preferences can change. Consider that non-Asians used to balk at eating sushi, or raw fish. In the twenty-first century, however, sushi has become common in grocery stores and restaurants across the United States, popular across all racial and ethnic groups. So perhaps tomorrow's US consumers will relish a grasshopper appetizer. Or so hope the guys at Exo and other entomophagists, or insect eaters. Grub Kitchen, a restaurant

"TODAY, 80% OF THE WORLD STILL EATS OVER 1,600 SPECIES OF INSECTS."
—Mark Sisson

FUTURE

At a food market in Bangkok, Thailand, a vendor sells fried scorpions, cockroaches, worms, grasshoppers, and other insects, which are popular snacks in Asia. The insect-as-food trend is slowly making its way to the United States and Europe.

in southern Wales in the United Kingdom, has been testing its insect-based dishes—such as cricket cookies, cumin cricket canapés, and roasted grubs— at pop-up eating events. Its chef, Andrew Holcroft, thinks that bug eating will be mainstream within the next ten to fifteen years.

Bugs will provide affordable sources of animal protein say the people at C-fu Foods. The company, based in Toronto, Ontario, in Canada, produces C-fu, a high-protein food made from mealworms. It looks like tofu and

DRINK THE DRINK

Some people eat primarily to live, with little interest in the taste and texture of food. One of these is the creator of a drink called Soylent. Rob Rhinehart, a software engineer from Atlanta, Georgia, was so utterly focused on his work that he wanted to eliminate buying and preparing food from his schedule. The product he developed in 2013 is a powder that he says provides complete nutrition. The ingredients are soybeans, oil derived from algae, a kind of sugar derived from beets, and vitamins and minerals. You simply mix the powder with water and drink it.

In his personal blog at robrhinehart.com, Rhinehart says that it's time humans move away from the traditional, often cruel farm-based ways of obtaining food toward what he calls "food as function." He writes, "The future of food is not the return to an agrarian [farming] society but the transcendence of [movement beyond] it. In time Soylent will be synthesized directly from light, water, and air with designer microorganisms. . . . I don't know who was the first farmer, but I want to be the last."

can be fried, sautéed, made into pâté, and added to soups. The folks at C-fu report that it takes about ten thousand mealworms to make about 1 pound (0.5 kg) of C-fu, which pound for pound has more protein than tofu. The company believes that bugs will help feed the world. They write, "The human population is expanding. By 2050 there will be 9 billion people on the planet. Researchers estimate it will require a 70–100% increase in our food production to sustain our burgeoning population. Insects can be part of the solution!" So far, the business is in its early stages and has not yet put C-fu on the shelves of grocery stores.

CUTTING EDGE

What else is trending? How about the 3D printing of food? In fact, some German nursing homes are already serving residents what appear to be chicken legs and side dishes of peas, cauliflower, potatoes, and pasta. But unlike many traditionally prepared meals, the 3D foods are soft and

This meal looks like chicken, green vegetables, and potatoes and tastes like chicken, green vegetables, and potatoes—because those are the ingredients. But the food has been cooked, blended, and remolded with a 3D printer into a meal that's easy to chew.

easy to chew. In earlier decades, elderly people who had trouble chewing or swallowing would eat baby food. With 3D food printing, they can eat soft foods that look and taste like the real thing—and are, in fact, made from the real thing. The chicken, vegetables, and other foods are cooked and pureed to a soft state, then molded by 3D printers into the form of the original food product.

High-tech approaches to growing food are also mushrooming. One is soil-free growing, or aeroponics, which involves raising plants in slightly misted air. A company named AeroFarms intends to grow 2 million pounds (907,000 kg) of greens such as kale, arugula, and lettuces in a vertical setup in Newark, New Jersey, using LED grow lights instead of sunshine. The seeds and then the plants are sprayed with the same kinds of nutrients

The company Sky Urban Solutions, in the Southeast Asian nation of Singapore, grows crops inside tall buildings. With aeroponic setups, farmers can grow food in crowded urban areas and sell it to nearby markets, with no need for long-distance shipping. And vertical farms take up little space at ground level, unlike the vast acreage covered by traditional farmland.

normally found in soils. Growing plants this way requires less than 10 percent of the water required by traditional methods. It also takes up less acreage.

Aquaculture refers to growing fish and other seafood in ponds or large tanks. Hydroponics refers to growing plants in water. Aquaponics combines the two approaches—and it can be done commercially on a large scale or even at home in your own living room. With an aquaponic setup, a producer can grow both plants and fish at the same time. The fish live in a water-filled tank. When that tank gets dirty with nutrient-rich fish waste, the dirty water is pumped into a flood tank. The nutrient-rich water from that tank drains into a hydroponic bed, providing nutrition for the plants growing there. The plants filter out nutrients from the waste-filled water and add oxygen (which plants give off during photosynthesis). This clean, oxygen-rich water drains back to the fish tank, providing a healthy environment for the fish.

Home delivery of food and juicing are not new, but a New York City–based company called Juicero has given it a new twist. Juicero, founded in 2013, not only will sell you a juicing machine but will also deliver to your home the freshest, locally grown (on their farms) produce to toss into the

FOOD DESIGN

Food design is a professional, futuristic field of work. It is not brand new, however. In 1915 a design team at the Root Glass Company of Terre Haute, Indiana, created the first Coke bottle, with its distinctive curvy shape—so distinctive, in fact, that even without its red-and-white logo on the label, you can tell it's a Coke bottle. In 1966 chemist and food storage designer Fredric J. Baur created the iconic tennis-ball-can packaging for Pringles potato chips.

But modern food design means more than the look of a box, bag, or bottle. Food itself is being imagined and then designed. A group in Italy has established the International Food Design Society. It aims to melt, pull, foam, mix, and reassemble "food as a raw material, transforming it to create something that did not exist before in terms of flavor, consistency, temperature, color and texture." The creators of the 3D-printed chicken and side dishes served in German nursing homes are examples of this type of food design.

Food design also encompasses packaging, the design of cooking tools, and the look of eating spaces. You can earn a degree in product design—and food can be the product—from the University of Minnesota in Minneapolis. The Food Studies Department at New York City's The New School offers courses in food design too.

machine. Plated, also out of New York, is another home delivery service. Founded in 2012, the company will bring you the makings for a meal, with recipe instructions included. The ingredients line up with the best in healthy eating. They are locally sourced, fresh, and sustainably raised. Other companies have jumped in, and it's likely that this trend may well put some personal chefs out of business.

THERE'S AN APP FOR THAT

As more and more people want to be better informed about what they eat, the apps world is responding. The designers of an app called Ingredient 1— developed in New York in 2014—say, "Our mission is to create transparency around food information, and make it easy for people to find the best foods for them. And to do that, we've launched an industry initiative around the collection and distribution of clean product data." With this app, you can explore foods that suit you, depending on your allergies, your desire for sustainability, and a range of other factors.

Other apps walk users through traditional grocery stores, revealing information about carb content product by product. One of these apps is InRFood, created in North Carolina. Its spinoff app, Sugar Cubes, shows you in pictures what 65 grams (2.3 ounces) of sugar in one 20-ounce (0.6-liter) bottle of Coke looks like, with visual comparisons to cubes, sugar packets, or teaspoons.

Providing an informative window into agriculture, Whole Foods Market installed an Instagram feed on a screen in the café of its store in Alpharetta, Georgia. The feed shows shoppers where their food is grown and how it looks while it's growing.

NEW FOODS

As people continue to look for healthy foods and tasty alternatives to meat, a wide range of new foods have popped up. For example, at your local grocery store or food coop, look for artisanal (handmade) local foods. Or see if you can find fermented products, such as sauerkraut and kimchi, which are filled with bacteria beneficial to the digestive system. Some nutritionists say that soybeans are healthier if eaten in fermented form, as in soy sauce and tempeh, rather than in highly processed faux (substitute) meats such as vegetarian bacon and hot dogs.

In the grocery store, also look for new or more nutritious takes on that old favorite—wheat. You're likely to see European-grown wheat or older, historic wheat varieties such as einkorn, kamut, emmer, and spelt. Other alternatives include farro, made from wheat berries, and the tiny cooked seeds of the ancient quinoa plant. Deborah Madison praises all the new options, many of which are actually riffs on foods that have been around for centuries. She writes,

Today you have almond milk, hemp, rice, coconut—all these non-dairy beverages. There are lots more possibilities for smoky flavors. . . . Now we have smoked paprika and smoked salt, even smoked tea. Ghee [butter with the milk proteins, sugars, and water removed] has suddenly become popular. It's not a new ingredient, just new to many of us. Or coconut oil, people are nuts about that. I love it, too.

Like bugs, some new foods might take some getting used to. Quorn is a meat substitute made from a fungus called *Fusarium venenatum*. The product is named after Quorn—the English village in which the fungus, a cousin to mushrooms, was identified. Quorn, the company, was launched in 1985 and produces a range of products resembling sausages, fillets, and other prepared meats (some of which have come under fire, as they may cause allergic reactions in some people).

A group in the Netherlands called Meat the Mushroom is taking shrimp shell waste, sterilizing and cooking it, and then placing the mix, along with some grain, into king oyster mushrooms. After two weeks on a shelf for fermentation, the result is what these innovators call cheese. It's a meat substitute.

YOU'RE YOUNG, SO GO DO SOMETHING

Teens who grew up watching the Food Network are no longer just hanging out at malls. Twenty-first-century kids are meeting in restaurants and lining up for tasty new fast food at food trucks.

And many of these young foodies know their way around a recipe. Romilly Newman, a New Yorker, taught herself to cook at the age of ten, started a blog called *Little Girl in the Kitchen* at eleven, and in 2012 appeared on the Food Network's show *Teen Chopped*. By high school, Newman was a well-established blogger and chef educator. Californian Flynn McGarry also started at the age of ten, inspired by *The French Laundry Cookbook*. By eleven he was turning out multicourse meals from his bedroom, which his filmmaker mom helped set up as a professional

With her HAPPY Organization, Haile Thomas, of Tuscon, Arizona, teaches other kids about cooking and healthy eating.

kitchen. By the age of seventeen, McGarry was studying with top chefs in major foodie cities such as New York, Seattle, and Los Angeles; was hosting pop-up food events at top restaurants; and had professional management.

A vegan chef putting her talents into educational and charitable projects, high schooler Haile Thomas works out of Tucson, Arizona. She was galvanized to explore vegetarian and vegan cooking when her father fell ill with diabetes. She founded a group called the HAPPY Organization in 2012. HAPPY stands for *h*ealthy *a*ctive *p*ositive *p*urposeful *y*outh. The group teaches kids to cook and encourages them to be physically active.

Many college students want their schools to serve healthy fare rather than processed food grown with chemicals and filled with preservatives. In 2007 a group of college students created the Real Food Challenge. Its goal is to persuade colleges to serve local, sustainable, and humanely raised food in student dining halls. One of the group's recent victories was at the University of Vermont, which after years of contracting with Sodexo, a major multinational food service company, agreed to take a new look at its contracts. A new deal being hammered out includes "a 2–3 year transition to a minimum of 40 percent locally or sustainably sourced ingredients, and a commitment to reach 70 percent sustainability levels by the end of a 10-year contract."

WHO, ME? VEGETARIAN?

Maybe you are interested in going veggie. If your family is very meat-and-potatoes oriented, it might be tough to convince them to make the change. One move is to volunteer to cook for the family. Busy parents—and siblings—may not even notice that their dinners have changed slightly when you start serving them tasty avocado and sautéed shitake mushroom tacos with green chili salsa or curry black bean veggie burgers on sourdough buns—especially if you do the dishes afterward.

Going hand in hand with cooking is an offer to help with some of the shopping. And it helps if you have all your facts in hand, so you can tell your family about health benefits, sustainability, animal cruelty, and other food-related issues.

If you're not ready to give up meat but want more fresh foods in your diet, some of the following moves might make sense to you:

- Persuade your family to buy produce from a CSA program.
- Invite your parents to join you on a weekly trip to a local farmers' market.
- Encourage your parents to buy more fruits and vegetables.

If your family can afford them, organic fruits and vegetables are excellent choices. But not everything you buy has to be organic. Or local. Many supermarket vegetables—picked fresh and quickly frozen—are relatively healthy choices. But if you don't buy organic fruits and vegetables, make sure to thoroughly wash and rinse your produce using vegetable-based soap. This will wash off any chemical residues that might remain from the farm.

Note that in almost every supermarket, the fresh vegetables and fruits, the dairy cases, the eggs and cheeses, the meat section, and the fish section are all on the outer edges. In the center of the supermarket, you'll find aisles of soft drinks, cookies, chips, crackers, canned foods, baked goods, and frozen dinners. This is the stuff to avoid.

LEARN, GROW, AND RAISE YOUR OWN

To get really serious and possibly save money for your family, demonstrate your own greens-growing skills by turning a nonproductive lawn into a food garden. Build some raised beds. These low rectangular structures, usually made of wood and filled with soil, will keep your garden contained, keep the soil depth even, and allow for good water control. Start with easy-to-grow plants such as lettuce, carrots, and onions. You can create a compost pile of vegetable kitchen scraps, leaves, and lawn cuttings in a separate bin or corner of the yard. After the material has decayed, you can spread it on your garden as fertilizer. You might also encourage the family to replace nondescript shrubs with edible landscaping, such as blueberry or currant or raspberry bushes.

If you don't have a yard, you might consider volunteering at a community garden. There you can learn about seeds, soil, irrigation, and other aspects of gardening. Some community gardens sell their produce to local shoppers. Others give the produce away for free. You can help either way. Or perhaps you can start a garden at your school or workplace, or on an empty lot in your town. A young CSA farmer in Boise, Idaho, wrote, "I may not be able to take down Monsanto [a big industrial agricultural company]. . . . But I can plant a seed, and so can you. Growing food— even a tomato in a pot on the balcony of an apartment—brings immense satisfaction and connection to something that's often overlooked in our increasingly urban population."

Many urban areas of the United States, typically poor neighborhoods, are called food deserts because they have few supermarkets. Many have only fast-food chains. According to the USDA, "About 2.3 million people

"GROWING FOOD—EVEN A TOMATO IN A POT ON THE BALCONY OF AN APARTMENT—BRINGS IMMENSE SATISFACTION AND CONNECTION TO SOMETHING THAT'S OFTEN OVERLOOKED IN OUR INCREASINGLY URBAN POPULATION."

—CSA farmer in Boise, Idaho

The city of Seattle, Washington, has set up eighty-eight P-Patch Community Gardens, where residents can grow their own food and learn about gardening.

(or 2.2 percent of all US households) live more than one mile [1.6 km] away from a supermarket and do not own a car." In response, some kids are working to bring healthy food to urban areas. One group of teens in San Antonio, Texas, built fifteen raised beds in their city, which they planted with corn, tomatoes, squash, peppers, beans, and herbs. The young people in the program carved out an oasis, a place of water and greenery and healthy food, right in the middle of their own food desert. At a harvest graduation ceremony, a local vegetarian chef made the participants tacos containing produce grown in the garden. Teens also used the produce to make their own healthy snacks in the kitchen of the Boys & Girls Club of San Antonio.

You might even consider becoming a guerrilla gardener, making seed balls out of wet soil and seeds, popping them into weedy spots around the neighborhood, and seeing what grows. Egg lovers? More and more towns and cities have removed legal barriers to raising hens in residential backyards. In some places, you can even rent a portable coop, some starter

You don't need a farm to raise chickens. These laying hens live in a coop in a neighborhood backyard in Los Angeles, California.

feed, and two hens. See what's available and legal in your community. But remember that raising hens is a commitment. You'll have to protect the birds from predators such as cats and raccoons; keep them fed; keep them warm or cool, depending on the season; clean their coops, and keep their water clean. To keep peace with the neighbors, try not to obtain an enthusiastically crowing rooster.

MAKING UP YOUR OWN MIND

You may have heard of ayurveda, an ancient healing tradition dating back to 5000 BCE in India. The word *ayurveda* means "the science of life." The ayurvedic dietary custom says that every meal we eat should cater to the six tastes. These tastes are sweet, sour, salty, pungent, bitter, and astringent (light and dry). Sweets can include grains and starchy vegetables. Green leafy vegetables can be bitter, while apples and lentils are astringent. People who adhere to ayurveda believe that if you eat from each of these taste-specific groups, your body will be satisfied.

EDGY VEGGIE

The term *vegetable forward* refers to a diet high in plant-based eating that doesn't totally shut the door on animal products. In a restaurant review in January 2015 in the *New York Observer,* writer Joshua David Stein describes the approach this way: "The [restaurant's] vegetable-heavy menu . . . is an outgrowth less of dogmatic adherence to vegetarianism than a realization of the waste inherent in the production and consumption of meat. Meat is present, but only at the margins, and treated as a precious resource."

Those who follow the three-thousand-year-old Chinese philosophy of the Tao, translated as "the way" or "the path," put enjoyment of life, balance, and simplicity above all else, believing in no rigid rules or dogma. They believe that chi, or universal life energy, flows through all living things, including us and what we eat. Taoists think that fresh, local food, with a balance of warm foods, such as chiles, and cool foods, such as dandelion greens, will keep you healthy. If you eat a combination of such foods, both animal- and vegetable-derived, you will be well fed, or so Taoists believe. Color, taste, and texture all come into play, and pondering these elements as we mindfully select, cook, and eat our meals will keep us well. A Taoist is unlikely to fret over food and plunge into the twenty-first century's newest eating disorder, *orthorexia nervosa* (Latin for "fixation on righteous eating" or, in plain English, a self-centered fanatical obsession with eating a pure, healthy, resist-all-temptation diet).

Becoming food-informed, evaluating what you think about food, making your own observations, and drawing your own conclusions based on all that information, plus relying on your own instincts, may be the way to go. The experts can offer guidance, but ultimately, you have to make up your own mind.

SOURCE NOTES

5 Joe Yonan, "Deborah Madison on 'New Vegetarian Cooking': 'I Want to Make It Resonate,'" *Washington Post*, May 23, 2014, http://www.washingtonpost.com/lifestyle /food/deborah-madison-on-new-vegetarian-cooking-i-want-to-make-it-resonate/2014/05 /22/d49085d6-e1d6-11e3-8dcc-d6b7fede081a_story.html.

5 Dennis Hughes, "Wholesome Cooking and Nutrition: An Interview with Mollie Katzen," Share Guide, accessed August 31, 2015, http://www.shareguide.com/Katzen.html.

6 "Happy Thanksgiving from CSPP," California School of Professional Psychology, November 24, 2014, http://csppblog.alliant.edu/cspp-blog/happy-thanksgiving-cspp -gratitude-resources-holiday/.

8 Alexandra Kleeman, "This Means Raw: Extreme Dieting and the Battle among Fruitarians," *Guardian* (Manchester), December 3, 2014, http://www.theguardian.com /news/2014/dec/03/-sp-trouble-with-fruitarians.

15 Jonathan Webb, "Oldest Human Faeces Show Neanderthals Ate Vegetables," *BBC News*, June 26, 2014, http://www.bbc.com/news/science-environment-27981702.

18 Jane Srivastava, "Vegetarianism and Meat-Eating in Eight Religions," *Hinduism Today*, April–June 2007, http://www.hinduismtoday.com/modules/smartsection/item.php? itemid=1541.

20 "Sri Guru Granth Sahib Translation," Sikhs.org, accessed August 31, 2015, http://www .sikhs.org/english/eg13.htm.

21 "Leviticus 11:1–17 English Standard Version," Bible Gateway, accessed August 31, 2015, https://www.biblegateway.com/passage/?search=Leviticus+11%3A1-17&version=ESV.

22 "Genesis 1:29," Bible Hub, accessed August 31, 2015, http://biblehub.com/genesis/1-29 .htm.

22 "Genesis 9:3," Bible Hub, accessed August 31, 2015, http://biblehub.com/genesis/9-3.htm.

24 Rita Laws, "Native Americans and Vegetarianism," IVU, accessed August 31, 2015, http://www.ivu.org/history/native_americans.html.

24 "Ancient Greece and Rose," International Vegetarian Union, accessed August 31, 2015, http://www.ivu.org/history/greece_rome/pythagoras.html.

25 Aristotle, "A Treatise on Government," Free Library, accessed August 31, 2015, http:// aristotle.thefreelibrary.com/A-Treatise-on-Government/1-8.

25 "History of Vegetarianism," International Vegetarian Union, accessed June 29, 2015, http://www.ivu.org/history/renaissance/mandeville.html.

25 Jeremy Bentham, "Jeremy Bentham on the Suffering of Non-Human Animals," Utilitarianism.com, accessed June 29, 2015, http://www.utilitarianism.com /jeremybentham.html.

25–26 Benjamin Franklin, "North America: 18th Century, Benjamin Franklin (1706–1790)," International Vegetarian Union, accessed June 29, 2015, http://www.ivu.org/history /northam18/franklin.html.

26 "Vegetarianism," Monticello, accessed June 29, 2015, https://www.monticello.org/site /research-and-collections/vegetarianism.

26 John Davis, "Extracts from Some Journals 1842–48—the Earliest Known Uses of the Word 'Vegetarian,'" International Vegetarian Union, accessed June 29, 2015, http://www .ivu.org/history/vegetarian.html.

27 Ibid.

27 "USA: 19th Century, Henry David Thoreau (1817–1862)," International Vegetarian Union, accessed June 29, 2015, http://www.ivu.org/history/usa19/thoreau.html.

30 "A Conversation with Plant Food Pioneer Mollie Katzen," Organic Connections Digital, accessed August 31, 2015, http://organicconnectmag.com/project/conversation-plant -food-pioneer-mollie-katzen/.

30–31 "Famous Vegetarians—Professor Peter Singer (1946–)," International Vegetarian Union, accessed August 13, 2015, http://www.ivu.org/people/writers/psinger.html.

32 "One Day a Week Can Make a World of Difference," Meat Free Monday, accessed August 31, 2015, http://www.meatfreemondays.com/.

33 "Anne Hathaway Swaps Vegan Diet for High Protein Paleo-Style Plan, Apologizes to PETA," Inquisitr, November 8, 2014, http://www.inquisitr.com/1594678/anne-hathaway -swaps-vegan-diet-for-high-protein-paleo-style-plan-apologizes-to-peta-video/.

33 Laura Hambleton, "Primatologist Jane Goodall, 77, Talks about How Chimps and Humans Age," Washington Post, December 5, 2011, http://www.washingtonpost.com/national /health-science/primatologist-jane-goodall-77-talks-about-how-chimps-and-humans -age/2011/11/28/gIQAmA7DWO_story.html.

37–38 Allison Aubrey, "Why We Got Fatter during the Fat-Free Food Boom," National Public Radio, March 28, 2014, http://www.npr.org/sections/thesalt/2014/03/28/295332576/why -we-got-fatter-during-the-fat-free-food-boom.

38 Nina Teicholz, The Big Fat Surprise (New York: Simon & Schuster, 2014), 2.

38 Ibid., 5.

38 Nina Teicholz, "The Questionable Link between Saturated Fat and Heart Disease," Wall Street Journal, May 6, 2014, http://www.wsj.com/news/articles/SB1000142405270230367 8404579533760760481486.

39 Susan Albers, "Eating Fabulous Food without Going Overboard," Psychology Today, August 19, 2013, https://www.psychologytoday.com/blog/comfort-cravings/201308 /eating-fabulous-food-without-going-overboard.

39 Mike Sager, "Julia Child: What I've Learned," *Esquire*, August 15, 2014, http://www.esquire.com/food-drink/interviews/a1273/julia-child-quotes-0601/.

39 Ibid.

40 Gary Taubes, *Good Calories, Bad Calories* (New York: Penguin, 2007), 454.

40 Andrew Weil, "Fat or Carbs: Which Is Worse," *Huffington Post*, November 17, 2011, http://www.huffingtonpost.com/andrew-weil-md/healthy-eating_b_629422.html.

40 Martha Rose Shulman, "Say Goodbye to 'Low Fat,'" *Zester Daily*, accessed August 31, 2015, http://zesterdaily.com/cooking/say-goodbye-to-low-fat/.

40 Ibid.

41 Nina Teicholz, "The Last Anti-Fat Crusaders," *Wall Street Journal*, October 28, 2014, http://www.wsj.com/articles/nina-teicholz-the-last-anti-fat-crusaders-1414536989.

41–42 Ibid.

42 Michael Wayne, "What the China Study Says about Eating Meat," Low Density Lifestyle, September 17, 2009, https://drmichaelwayne.com/health-and-wellness/health-and-wellness/diet-and-nutrition/page/4/.

42 Alona Pulde and Matthew Lederman, *The Forks over Knives Plan* (New York: Touchstone, 2014), 4–5.

43 Tom Naughton, "Outstanding Critique of the China Study," Fat Head, July 13, 2010, http://www.fathead-movie.com/index.php/2010/07/13/outstanding-critique-of-the-china-study/.

43 "Why Go Vegan," Vegan.com, accessed August 31, 2015, http://www.vegan.com/why/.

44 Kris Gunnars, "Top 11 Biggest Lies about Vegan Diets," Authority Nutrition, accessed August 31, 2015, http://authoritynutrition.com/top-11-biggest-lies-about-vegan-diets/.

45 Georgia Ede, "Vegetables," Diagnosis: Diet, accessed June 29, 2015, http://www.diagnosisdiet.com/food/vegetables/.

46 "You Want Facts?," Real Meal Revolution, accessed August 31, 2015, http://realmealrevolution.com/the-facts.

47 Barbara Griggs, "The Rise and Rise of Sourdough Bread," *Guardian* (Manchester), August 12, 2014, http://www.theguardian.com/lifeandstyle/2014/aug/12/rise-sourdough-bread-slow-fermented-health-benefits.

49 Daniel Kline, "Will Replacing High Fructose Corn Syrup with Real Sugar Help Pepsi?," Motley Fool, April 10, 2014, http://www.fool.com/investing/general/2014/04/10/will-replacing-high-fructose-corn-syrup-with-real.aspx.

49 Ibid.

49 Marion Nestle, "Food Politics 10th Anniversary," Responsible Eating and Living, June 4, 2013, http://responsibleeatingandliving.com/?page_id=11066.

49 Zoe Williams, "Robert Lustig: The Man Who Believes Sugar Is Poison," *Guardian* (Manchester), August 24, 2014, http://www.theguardian.com/lifeandstyle/2014/aug/24/robert-lustig-sugar-poison.

51 Deborah Madison, *Vegetable Literacy* (Berkeley, CA: Ten Speed, 2013), 4.

52 Mark Bittman, "Let Them Eat Foie Gras," *New York Times*, January 13, 2015.

53 Eric Pianin, "How Billions in Tax Dollars Subsidize the Junk Food Industry," *Business Insider*, July 25, 2012, http://www.businessinsider.com/billions-in-tax-dollars-subsidize-the-junk-food-ind ustry-2012-7.

53–54 Jonathan Foley, "It's Time to Rethink America's Corn System," *Scientific American*, March 5, 2013, http://www.scientificamerican.com/article/time-to-rethink-corn/.

55 Jorge Fernandez-Cornejo, Seth Wechsler, Mike Livington, and Lorraine Mitchell, "Genetically Engineered Crops in the United States," USDA, accessed August 31, 2015, http://www.ers.usda.gov/media/1282246/err162.pdf.

56 David Schubert, "The Coming Food Disaster," *CNN*, January 28, 2015, http://www.cnn.com/2015/01/27/opinion/schubert-herbicides-crops/index.htmlhttp.

56–57 Michael Moss, "Lawmakers Aim to Protect Farm Animals in U.S. Research," *New York Times*, February 5, 2015, http://www.nytimes.com/2015/02/05/dining/lawmakers-aim-to-protect-farm-animals-in-us-research.html.

58 Tom Philpott, "How the Midwest's Corn Farms Are Cooking the Planet," *Mother Jones*, August 12, 2016, http://www.motherjones.com/tom-philpott/2015/08/how-midwests-corn-farms-are-cooking-planet.

62–63 Berlin Reed, *The Ethical Butcher* (Berkeley, CA: Soft Skull Press, 2013), 119–120.

63 Reed, *Ethical Butcher*, 52.

63 Ibid., xxiii.

65 Anna Lappé "Five Amazing Things I Learned from the World's Leaders of the Organic Food Movement," *Anna Lappé*, December 1, 2014, http://annalappe.com/2014/12/5-amazing-things-i-learned-from-the-worlds-leaders-of-the-organic-food-movement/.

66 Barry Yeoman, "The Organic Food Paradox," *Saturday Evening Post*, March/April 2012, http://www.saturdayeveningpost.com/2012/03/06/in-the-magazine/trends-and-opinions/the-organic-food-paradox.html.

67 Ibid.

67 Cinda S. Chima, "Nutri Q & A," University of Akron, accessed June 29, 2015, http://www3.uakron.edu/chima/text/Food percent20storage percent20article percent208-05.pdf.

68 Ibid.

68 "Why Crickets?," Exo, accessed August 31, 2015, https://www.exoprotein.com/why-crickets.

70 Rob Rhinehart, "Soylent Raises Money," Mostly Harmless, January 15, 2015, http://robrhinehart.com/?p=1192.

70 "Why C-fu," C-fu Foods, accessed June 29, 2015, http://cfufoods.com/why-c-fu/.

73 "Food Design," International Food Design Society, accessed August 31, 2015, http://ifooddesign.org/food_design/subcategories.php.

73-74 "Mission," Ingredient 1, accessed August 31, 2015, http://www.ingredient1.com/mission.html.

75 Joe Yonan, "Deborah Madison on 'New Vegetarian Cooking': 'I Want to Make It Resonate,'" Washington Post, May 23, 2014, http://www.washingtonpost.com/lifestyle/food/deborah-madison-on-new-vegetarian-cooking-i-want-to-make-it-resonate/2014/05/22/d49085d6-e1d6-11e3-8dcc-d6b7fede081a_story.html.

76 "Home," Meat Free Monday, accessed August 31, 2015, http://www.meatfreemondays.com/.

78 Casey, "Ted Talk: Seeds and the Abundant Economy," Earthly Delights Farm, January 20, 2015, http://earthlydelightsfarm.com/ted-talk-seeds-and-the-abundant-economy/.

78 Ibid.

78-79 "Food Deserts," Food Empowerment Project, accessed June 29, 2015, http://www.foodispower.org/food-deserts/.

81 Joshua David Stein, "At Semilla, a 'Vegetable-Forward' Menu Points the Way to Mindful Eating," New York Observer, January 20, 2015, http://observer.com/2015/01/at-semilla-a-vegetable-forward-menu-points-the-way-to-mindful-eating/.

GLOSSARY

biodiversity: the variety of organisms living in an environment. Biodiversity in agriculture involves rotating crops in the same field from season to season. By planting corn (which takes a lot of nitrogen from the soil) one season, followed by soybeans (which puts nitrogen back into soil) the next season, farmers can help their soil stay healthy.

carbohydrate: one of three main types of nutrients that provide energy to the body. (The others are proteins and fats.) Simple carbohydrates are found in sweeteners such as table sugar, honey, and corn syrup, as well as in fruits. They provide the body with a quick burst of energy. Complex carbohydrates contain fiber, which the body digests more slowly. Sources of complex carbohydrates include carrots, potatoes, beans, wheat, and other grains.

carnivore: a person, animal, or plant that exclusively eats meat

cholesterol: a fatty substance made in the human liver and also found in meat, egg yolks, butter, cheese, and some plants. Cholesterol helps the body digest food, create hormones, and produce vitamin D. Low-density lipoprotein (LDL) is commonly called bad cholesterol. Coming from trans fats, carbohydrates, and certain oils, such as soy, corn, peanut, and almond oil, LDL is linked to heart disease. High-density lipoprotein (HDL) is often called good cholesterol because it removes LDL cholesterol from the bloodstream. Foods that boost HDL cholesterol include soy, nuts, and beans.

climate change: an increase in temperatures on Earth, caused by increased levels of carbon dioxide in Earth's atmosphere. With more carbon dioxide, Earth's atmosphere traps more sunlight, thereby warming the planet. The excess carbon dioxide comes from the burning of fossil fuels (petroleum, coal, and natural gas).

community supported agriculture (CSA): programs in which families and restaurants pay farms at the beginning of the growing season and then receive regular deliveries of fresh farm produce throughout the season

compost: organic material created from decayed leaves, grass, plant-based kitchen waste, and other plant material. Many farmers and gardeners apply compost to their soil because it provides nutrients to soil and to growing plants.

corn syrup: a thick liquid sweetener made from corn. Food manufacturers use corn syrup to sweeten many snacks, soft drinks, and other food products.

diabetes: a long-term chronic disease that disrupts the body's ability to use glucose, a type of sugar. If left untreated, diabetes leads to a high concentration of glucose in the blood, which can cause health problems such as blindness, kidney failure, heart attack, and stroke. Diabetes can take one of two forms. Type 1 diabetes, which usually develops during childhood, results from the destruction of insulin-producing cells in the pancreas. Without insulin, the body cannot process glucose, which then builds up in the bloodstream. Type 2 diabetes, which occurs most often in middle-aged and elderly adults, develops when the body doesn't produce enough insulin and doesn't process it properly. Doctors have linked Type 2 diabetes to obesity and insufficient exercise.

domestication: the conditioning of plants and animals to live alongside humans, for the benefit of humans. Domesticating plants involves selecting desirable species, breeding them, and growing them as agricultural crops. Domesticating animals involves taming, protecting, and breeding certain species, which can then provide humans with milk, meat, eggs, wool, and other products.

drought: an extended period of little or no rainfall, especially one that causes farm crops to wither and die

ethanol: an alcohol that can be derived from corn and other plants and that is often used to power vehicles. Encouraged by government incentive programs, many US farmers devote large portions of their corn crop to ethanol production and much less to food production.

ethics: standards of behavior concerning what a person or group of people believe to be right and wrong

factory farming: raising large numbers of livestock in indoor facilities, with mechanically controlled systems of feeding and watering, and with a high reliance on hormone- and antibiotic-enhanced feed. Factory farming allows livestock producers to raise and bring many animals to market quickly.

fats: one of three main types of nutrients that provide energy to the body. (The others are proteins and carbohydrates.) Fats come from both plant and animal foods. Fats insulate the human body, keep the brain working well, give the body energy, and help rebuild cells.

fermentation: a biological process that preserves food, changes its form, or enhances its flavor—or all three. The process is carried out by microbes such as bacteria, mold, or yeast. Examples of fermentation include grain turning into beer and milk turning into cheese or yogurt.

fertilizer: material added to soil to promote plant growth. Organic fertilizers include decayed plant matter (compost) and animal waste. Inorganic fertilizers come from minerals or chemicals, such as nitrogen and phosphorus.

forager: a person or animal that gathers wild plants or animals for food. Early humans obtained much of their food by foraging.

fossil fuels: energy-providing materials formed deep underground from the long-dead remains of ancient plants and animals. Fossil fuels include coal, petroleum, and natural gas. The burning of fossil fuels releases high levels of carbon dioxide into Earth's atmosphere, which has led to climate change on Earth.

genetic engineering: the process of altering deoxyribonucleic acid (DNA), a substance that determines an organism's characteristics, to change that organism in some positively perceived way. In agriculture, scientists use genetic engineering to create plants or animals with desirable traits, such as insect-resistant corn and beef cattle with lean meat.

gluten: a combination of proteins found in certain grains (including wheat, rye, and barley) that gives dough made from their flours stickiness and elasticity. Some people—those who have celiac disease—cannot eat gluten because it damages their intestines. Gluten can also cause less serious gastrointestinal problems, such as bloating, in people without celiac disease. These people are said to be gluten-sensitive.

herbivore: an animal whose diet is made up only of plant material, such as leaves, grasses, and other greens

irrigation: the application of water, other than natural rainfall, to land being used to grow crops. Farmers use pumps, canals, dams, and other devices and structures to manage irrigation waters and to direct them to crops.

locavore: a person who eats primarily food that is grown or produced in the area where that person lives

monoculture: the agricultural practice of growing the same crop on the same ground year after year. Monoculture can deplete the soil of nutrients. It also leaves farms vulnerable to having an entire crop wiped out by a single pest or disease.

omnivore: a person or animal that eats a diet of plants, fish, shellfish, dairy products, and meat

organic food: food grown without inorganic fertilizers, chemical pesticides, or genetically modified seeds, usually on land cultivated with sustainable agricultural practices

pescatarian: a person who eats fish but does not eat other kinds of meat

pesticide: a substance used to repel or kill insects, microbes, animals, or plants that might harm crops

protein: one of three main types of nutrients that provide energy to the body. (The others are carbohydrates and fats.) Proteins are made of amino acids. They help build, maintain, and repair body tissue and also keep body systems functioning properly. Proteins come from meat, fish, dairy products, eggs, nuts, beans, potatoes, and sweet potatoes. Some fruits and green veggies, such as avocados and broccoli, also provide protein.

saturated fat: the fat contained naturally in meats, cheeses, butter, nuts, and olive and coconut oils

subsidy: money paid to a farm or other company, usually by a government, to encourage certain activity. For instance, the US government gives subsidies to farmers to grow corn for ethanol, a fuel that is less harmful to the environment than fossil fuels.

sustainable agriculture: farming techniques that do not permanently damage the land or permanently deplete natural resources

trans-unsaturated fats: solid fats created from liquid oils through manufacturing. Also known as trans fats, these fats are linked to heart disease and other health problems. In 2015 the US Food and Drug Administration instituted a three-year phase out of trans fats in commercial food products.

vegan: a person who eats no meats or animal products of any kind, including dairy foods or eggs. Many vegans do not wear clothing or use products made from leather, wool, or other materials derived from animals.

vegetarian: a person who does not eat meat but may eat dairy products and eggs

SELECTED BIBLIOGRAPHY

Aubrey, Allison. "Why We Got Fatter during the Fat-Free Food Boom." *National Public Radio*, March 28, 2014. http://www.npr.org/sections/thesalt/2014/03/28/295332576/why-we-got -fatter-during-the-fat-free-food-boom.

Bittman, Mark. "Let Them Eat Foie Gras." *New York Times*, January 13, 2015.

———. *VB6: Eat Vegan before 6:00*. New York: Clarkson Potter, 2013.

"A Conversation with Plant Food Pioneer Mollie Katzen." Organic Connections Digital. Accessed February 15, 2015. http://organicconnectmag.com/project/conversation-plant-food-pioneer -mollie-katzen/.

Fernandez-Cornejo, Jorge, Seth Wechsler, Mike Livington, and Lorraine Mitchell. "Genetically Engineered Crops in the United States." USDA, February 2014. http://www.ers.usda.gov /media/1282246/err162.pdf.

Foley, Jonathan. "It's Time to Rethink America's Corn System." *Scientific American*, March 5, 2013. http://www.scientificamerican.com/article/time-to-rethink-corn/.

Kassoff, Anya. *The Vibrant Table*. Boston: Roost Books, 2014.

Lappé, Anna. "Five Amazing Things I Learned from the World's Leaders of the Organic Food Movement." *Anna Lappé*, December 1, 2014. http://annalappe.com/2014/12/5-amazing -things-i-learned-from-the-worlds-leaders-of-the-organic-food-movement/.

Lappé, Frances Moore. *Food First*. New York: Ballantine Books, 1978.

Levenstein, Harvey. *Fear of Food*. Chicago: University of Chicago Press, 2012.

Lurie, Julie. "California's Almonds Suck as Much Water Annually as Los Angeles Uses in Three Years." *Mother Jones*, January 12, 2015. http://www.motherjones.com/environment/2015/01 /almonds-nuts-crazy-stats-charts.

Morison, Carole. "Dispelling the Myths." Food for Thought. Accessed June 29, 2015. https:// oldfarmerlady.wordpress.com/.

Moss, Michael. "Lawmakers Aim to Protect Farm Animals in U.S. Research. *New York Times*, February 5, 2015. http://www.nytimes.com/2015/02/05/dining/lawmakers-aim-to-protect -farm-animals-in-us-research.html.

Nestle, Marion. "Food Politics 10th Anniversary." Responsible Eating and Living, June 4, 2013. http://responsibleeatingandliving.com/?page_id=11066.

Petersen, Grant. *Eat Bacon, Don't Jog*. New York: Workman, 2014.

Pianin, Eric. "How Billions in Tax Dollars Subsidize the Junk Food Industry." *Business Insider*, July 25, 2012. http://www.businessinsider.com/billions-in-tax-dollars-subsidize-the-junk -food-ind ustry-2012-7.

Pulde, Alona, and Matthew Lederman. *The Forks over Knives Plan*. New York: Touchstone, 2014.

Sager, Mike. "Julia Child: What I've Learned." *Esquire*, August 15, 2014. http://www.esquire.com /food-drink/interviews/a1273/julia-child-quotes-0601/.

Schubert, David. "The Coming Food Disaster." *CNN*, January 28, 2015. http://www.cnn.com/2015 /01/27/opinion/schubert-herbicides-crops/index.htmlhttp.

Shulman, Martha Rose. "Say Goodbye to 'Low Fat.'" *Zester Daily*. Accessed February 15, 2015. http://zesterdaily.com/cooking/say-goodbye-to-low-fat/.

Taubes, Gary. *Good Calories, Bad Calories*. New York: Penguin, 2007.

——. *Why We Get Fat*. New York: Knopf, 2011.

Teicholz, Nina. *The Big Fat Surprise*. New York: Simon & Schuster, 2014.

——. "The Last Anti-Fat Crusaders." *Wall Street Journal*, October 28, 2014. http://www.wsj.com /articles/nina-teicholz-the-last-anti-fat-crusaders-1414536989.

Tristram, Stuart. *The Bloodless Revolution*. New York: W. W. Norton, 2007.

Weil, Andrew. "Fat or Carbs: Which Is Worse?" *Huffington Post*, November 17, 2011. http://www .huffingtonpost.com/andrew-weil-md/healthy-eating_b_629422.html.

Williams, Zoe. "Robert Lustig: The Man Who Believes Sugar Is Poison." *Guardian* (Manchester), August 24, 2014. http://www.theguardian.com/lifeandstyle/2014/aug/24/robert-lustig-sugar-poison.

Yeoman, Barry. "The Organic Food Paradox." *Saturday Evening Post*, March/April 2012. http:// www.saturdayeveningpost.com/2012/03/06/in-the-magazine/trends-and-opinions/the -organic-food-paradox.html.

FOR FURTHER INFORMATION

BOOKS

Belasco, Warren. *Meals to Come: A History of the Future of Food*. Berkeley: University of California Press, 2006.

Child, Julia. *Mastering the Art of French Cooking: 50th Anniversary*. New York: Alfred A. Knopf, 2001.

Gay, Kathlyn. *Food: The New Gold*. Minneapolis: Twenty-First Century Books, 2013.

Hand, Carol. *Dead Zones: Why Earth's Waters Are Losing Oxygen*. Minneapolis: Twenty-First Century Books, 2016.

Kallen, Stuart A. *Running Dry: The Global Water Crisis*. Minneapolis: Twenty-First Century Books, 2015.

Katzen, Mollie. *Moosewood Cookbook: 40th Anniversary Edition*. Emeryville, CA: Ten Speed, 2014.

Madison, Deborah. *Vegetable Literacy: Cooking and Gardening with Twelve Families from the Edible Plant Kingdom*. Berkeley, CA: Ten Speed, 2013.

Pollan, Michael. *Cooked: A Natural History of Transformation.* New York: Penguin, 2013.

———. *The Omnivore's Dilemma: The Secrets behind What You Eat.* Young Readers edition. Saint Louis, MO: Turtleback Books, 2009.

Reed, Berlin. *The Ethical Butcher.* Berkeley, CA: Soft Skull, 2013.

Simon, David Robinson. *Meatonomics.* Newburyport, MA: Conari, 2013.

Thomas, Haile. *The Supernatural Kids Cookbook.* Los Angeles: Huqua, 2013.

Warren, Rachel Meltzer. *The Smart Girl's Guide to Going Vegetarian.* Naperville, IL: Sourcebooks 2014.

Zachos, Ellen. *Backyard Foraging.* North Adams, MA: Storey, 2013.

WEBSITES

Authority Nutrition
http://www.authoritynutrition.com
This website aims to clearly explain the science behind sensible food choices, with information based on random clinical trials, not assumptions. The site is run by nutrition researcher Kris Gunnars, a nutrition researcher.

Dining with Flynn
http://www.diningwithflynn.com
On this website, teen chef Flynn McGarry provides sample menus and details about Eureka, a supper club that he runs out of his mother's home in Los Angeles. The site also includes links to media reports on Flynn.

Humane Farm Animal Care (HFAC)
http://www.certifiedhumane.org
HFAC is dedicated to improving the lives of farm animals raised for food, from birthing to slaughtering. The organization provides information for consumers looking for food products from humanely raised animals, with additional information on the organizations programs and goals.

Meatless Monday
http://www.meatlessmonday.com
The Meatless Monday organization encourages people to give up meat one day per week for physical health, to save money, and to help preserve Earth's resources. The website explains the benefits of eating less meat, provides recipes, and discusses the organization's work around the globe.

Nom Nom Paleo
http://www.nomnompaleo.com
This lively, humor-filled, and well-illustrated site explains paleo diets and offers recipes, videos, and other resources for those interested in eating the way our prehistoric ancestors might have done.

Organic Consumers Association (OCA)
  http://www.organicconsumers.org
  OCA is dedicated to converting more US farmland to organic agriculture, reducing subsidies for industrial farms, halting the production of genetically engineered foods, and ending dangerous industrial and factory farming practices. The website describes the organization's work.

Real Food Challenge
  http://www.realfoodchallenge.org
  Real Food Challenge is an organization of young people working to bring healthy food to their universities and communities. The website describes the group's programs and tells how to get involved.

Vegan.com
  http://www.vegan.com
  This extensive website offers lots of resources for vegans, including recipes, book reviews, and nutritional information.

Vegetarian Resource Group
  http://www.vrg.org
  Here you'll find a full cornucopia of information about vegetarianism, including recipes, lists of vegetarian restaurants, and articles on nutrition and animal rights.

World Food Programme (WFP)
  http://www.wfp.org/hunger
  The World Food Programme (WFP), operated by the United Nations, notes that nearly eight hundred million people on Earth are undernourished. The WFP website provides statistics and other information about hunger and malnutrition and describes its global work to alleviate hunger.

FILMS

Fed Up. DVD. Santa Monica, CA: Atlas Films, 2014.
  This documentary puts the spotlight on sugar and its role in causing obesity in the United States. The film also debunks the notion that exercise, while good for us, is the key to losing weight.

Food, Inc. DVD. New York: Magnolia Pictures, 2008.
  The filmmakers examine how multinational corporations control the US food industry. They also explore issues of human health, the environmental impacts of corporate farming, and the treatment of animals on factory farms.

Food Chains. DVD. New York: Illumine, 2014.
  This film examines the lives of the migrant laborers who harvest our food, under challenging conditions and for low pay.

Forks over Knives. DVD. Santa Monica, CA: Monica Beach Media, 2011.
  This film promotes veganism for health, urging people to switch from an animal- and junk-food-based diet to an entirely plant-based one.

INDEX

PHOTO ACKNOWLEDGMENTS

The images in this book are used with the permission of: © iStockphoto.com/Georgijevic, p. 7; © H. Armstrong Roberts/Retrofile Creative/Getty Images, p. 10; © Roger de la Harpe/Gallo Images/Getty Images, p. 12; © Kennan Ward/Corbis, p. 13; © Reuters/Corbis, p. 17; © Indian School, (18th century)/Private Collection/Christie's Images/Bridgeman Images, p. 19; © Werner Forman/Universal Images Group/Getty Images, p. 23; © Health Exhibits, p. 28; © Swim Ink 2, LLC/Corbis, p. 29; © Saul Loeb/AFP/Getty Images, p. 31; © Kevin Mazur/VF15/WireImage/Getty Images, p. 33; James F. Quinn/KRT/Newscom, p. 37; © New York Times Co./Getty Images, p. 39; © ChinaFotoPress/Getty Images, p. 41; USDA, p. 44; © Zigy Kaluzny/Stone/Getty Images, p. 46; © Joe Raedle/Getty Images, p. 48; Pete Souza/KRT/Newscom, p. 52; © Geography Photos/Universal Images Group/Getty Images, p. 55; © Deyan Georgiev/Alamy, p. 59; © Alan Franzluebbers/USDA, p. 62; © Andrew TB Tan/flickr Editorial/Getty Images, p. 69; AP Photo/Rex Features , p. 71; AP Photo/Kyodo, p. 73; Courtesy of Rosalinda Rachel Photography, p. 76; © Paul Gordon/Alamy, p. 79; © Danita Delimont/Gallo Images/Getty Images, p. 80.

Cover © iStockphoto.com/Serg_Velusceac (fruits and vegetables); © iStockphoto.com/a-poselenov (cow).

ABOUT THE AUTHOR

Meredith Sayles Hughes is the author of Plants We Eat, a series of ten books about food plants; *The Great Potato Book*; and, with Tom Hughes, *Gastronomie: Food Museums and Heritage Sites of France.* She is cofounder of two online museums: the Potato Museum (imagehost.net/potatomuseum/index.html) and the Food Museum (foodmuseum.com). Hughes has written food blogs, presented food history workshops, and developed museum exhibits and educational programming about food. She lives in Albuquerque, New Mexico.